PATRIOT PRIDE

My Life in the New England Dynasty

PATRIOT PRIDE

MY LIFE IN THE NEW ENGLAND DYNASTY

Troy Brown
with
Mike Reiss

TRIUMPH
BOOKS

To my mother, Richadean,
for teaching me to become a man.

To my children, Sir'mon, SaanJay, and Skylar,
for making me become an even better man and
continuing to be my driving inspiration.

ooooo

Library of Congress Cataloging-in-Publication Data available upon request.

This book is available in quantity at special discounts for your group or organization. For further information, contact:

Triumph Books
814 North Franklin Street
Chicago, Illinois 60610
Phone: (312) 337-0747
Fax: (312) 280-5470
www.triumphbooks.com

Printed in U.S.A.

ISBN: 978-1-62937-521-2
Design by Meghan Grammer
Photos courtesy of AP Images except where otherwise noted.

CONTENTS

FOREWORD

As a member of the New England Patriots for the last 16 years, it has been a privilege to be teammates with some of the NFL's best players who have become friends for life. Troy Brown is certainly in that category.

When I joined the Patriots in 2000 as a sixth-round draft choice out of Michigan, Troy had already been with the franchise for seven years. It was probably seven years longer than many thought he would stick around based on his draft status, but it was easy for me to see why he had such staying power. He was one of the team's hardest workers, humble, a great competitor, and he always put the team first. He was a great example for a rookie like me to follow.

Add in Troy's natural skills as a wide receiver—how he always seemed to have a knack for being in the right place at the right time, using his quickness, intelligence and uncanny vision to get open—and it highlights how he was a critical part of the foundation of our Super Bowl championship teams in 2001, 2003, and 2004. In my first year as a starting quarterback in 2001, I would sometimes think to myself, "When in doubt, get it to Troy."

Defenses always had to be conscious of where Troy was on the field. As a quarterback, the things I most appreciated were his dependability and consistency. He ran great routes, had great hands, and a great general awareness of what was happening around him. He added a steadying presence to our wide receiver corps.

Looking back, when I think about some of the memorable plays Troy delivered, it is difficult to pick one that stands out above the rest. There are so many.

His 23-yard catch on the final drive against the St. Louis Rams in Super XXXVI was the type of clutch play he was known for, as he got out of bounds to stop the clock and set up the game-winning field goal. He was always so smart.

Some said Troy couldn't threaten a defense down the field, but his 82-yard touchdown catch in overtime against the Miami Dolphins in 2003 showed that wasn't the case. It was a slant and he left everyone on defense in the dust at a time when players were physically and mentally exhausted. Troy was always so mentally tough, and that's what it took because at the time we had a 0–13 record in South Florida in games played in September and October.

It was always great having Troy in the offensive huddle, and the defense found that to be the case as well. Watching him switch to cornerback in 2004, and total three interceptions that year, was a perfect example of how he always put the team first. Those defensive skills came in handy in the 2006 playoffs when he kept our season alive by stripping San Diego Chargers safety Marlon McCree after an interception.

And, of course, Troy's contributions on special teams were exemplary.

Sometimes you hear people say "he did it all for his team" and it's a bit of an overstatement. But with Troy, he truly did it all—offense, defense, and special teams.

I remember being asked about Troy in the 2004 season when his selfless switch to defense was a big storyline around our team, and this is what I said: "He has respect from everybody. He is very coachable and has a great attitude. He is what this team is all about—tough, smart, and he works his butt off."

Like many others, I view Troy as one of the greatest players in the history of the franchise, which is evidenced by his 2012 induction into the team's Hall of Fame. He was a great playmaker and leader on the field and a top-notch teammate off the field. He had a way of bringing people together, even though he wasn't always the type to deliver a motivational-type speech.

Troy has had great success in his post-playing career, which is no surprise, and he has remained one of my close friends through the years. I am honored that he asked me to participate in this book that chronicles his career from pee-wee football to the NFL, and sends a message to youngsters that even a longshot underdog can achieve greatness if they stay true to themselves, work hard, and put the team first.

We had a lot of great memories together, and I'm excited that you'll now have a chance to go behind the scenes with Troy to relive that special time in our lives, and even beyond that to learn more about Troy's remarkable journey.

—**Tom Brady**
June 2015

INTRODUCTION

He caught the ball on his back! Wait, did he just catch the ball on his back?

Yes, he did.

That was one of my first memories of Troy Brown with the New England Patriots. It pretty much summed up Troy as a football player: Don't underestimate his ability to come through with the most improbable play when his team needed it the most.

On the final day of the 1996 NFL season, I was sitting in the stands at Giants Stadium, one of the 65,387 in attendance to see if the Patriots could secure a victory and earn a coveted first-round playoff bye. As a fan, it was depressing to see them fall behind 22–0 at halftime. They needed a spark and of course it was Troy who would deliver it.

The Patriots came roaring back in the second half to record a 23–22 win, the margin for error razor thin as they faced a third-and-13 situation on their game-winning drive. That's when Troy Brown made one of the unforgettable plays in that era of Patriots football, a diving-on-his-back-and-stretching-out-his-body reception for 13 yards.

They needed 13. Troy got the 13.

As I transitioned from fan to young professional/football reporter the following year, it was my pleasure to follow the rest of Troy's career from the perspective of Patriots reporter. I came to know him as a quiet leader and a shining example of how when the odds are stacked against you, it doesn't mean you can't win.

Troy Brown won. He won big. He shined on the grandest stages of professional football and did whatever the team needed, from catching the ball as a receiver, to returning punts, and ultimately switching to the cornerback position in the 2004 Super Bowl season when the team had a run of unfortunate injuries.

What you're about to read is his story, from humble beginnings in Blackville, South Carolina, to three-time Super Bowl champion and Patriots Hall of Fame player (1993–2007). It's an underdog story because eighth-round draft choices from Marshall University aren't supposed to make it in the NFL. Perhaps you've noticed, but they don't even have an eighth round in the NFL Draft anymore.

When Troy approached me about telling his story, his hope was that a young student might read it and be inspired. I hopped on board quickly, because as a father of two young children, this is the type of story I want them to read.

You're not supposed to be able to catch a football flat on your back when the game is on the line. You're also not supposed to go from wide receiver to cornerback and intercept three passes that season.

Then again, as Troy proved over and over again, anything is possible.

—Mike Reiss
April 2015

One

MODEST BEGINNINGS IN BLACKVILLE, SOUTH CAROLINA

Those were the times when he would think
back to Blackville and say to himself,
"Every little crumb, every little
thing, just appreciate it."

CHAPTER ONE

Modest Beginnings in Blackville, South Carolina

This is where the journey began: Blackville, South Carolina.

To call it a modest beginning would be an understatement. In a town of about 2,000 residents, Troy's home was an itsy-bitsy ranch with a few walls that divided the space into multiple rooms to provide some form of privacy. But considering how many people were packed into the home, there was really no privacy at all. No closets, either. Everyone's clothes and belongings were stored in footlockers at the foot of the bed and those footlockers made for nice stools to sit on, too.

In football, they'd call this the bunch formation. Everyone packed in tight.

The leader of the house was Troy's grandmother, who in many ways was the best coach he ever had. Troy would later play for two of the all-time great football coaches in Bill Parcells and Bill Belichick, but there was no one like Grandma Wilhamenia. She had nine children, the second oldest of whom was Troy's mother. All of them, and their kids, lived together in the small home.

So Grandma Wilhamenia not only raised her own kids, she basically raised her grandchildren too. She was Troy's first true role model.

Life wasn't easy for the family in Blackville, South Carolina, at the time. To make sure they had this modest roof over their head, they worked in the fields—the vast acreage around the house that had animals such as chickens running around the backyard—in exchange for shelter. Part of the work included picking cotton. No, there weren't video games to be played.

There were basically four rooms in the house—one for the girls, one for the boys, with a wooden swinging door separating them. Things were more cramped in the boys' room, with six of them there at one point before some left for the military. The three girls had a bit more space, but not much more.

Grandma Wilhamenia's room was on the other side, which also served as the family room. A small kitchen and washroom was behind that.

The bathroom was in the backyard—an outhouse 20 to 30 yards from the home. One time, during a storm, it blew away. That turned out to be a good thing because the new outhouse had two bowls, depending on what you had to do. Talk about luxury.

Friends described Troy's home as "Little House on the Prairie." Looking out the front door, one could see a distribution area across the field where 18-wheeler trucks would line up to be stocked with produce. It was rural. Real rural.

In the fields, Troy would chop wood and pick peanuts and corn. When you're four years old, there is a certain acceptance to this being the way life is. It just seemed normal.

He later learned otherwise. This is why Troy is so appreciative of the life that football has provided him; it starts in Blackville. That's where he learned that everything you get in life is earned. It's where he learned sacrifice. It's where he learned that words can sometimes ring hollow; it's the actions that count: If you don't work in the fields, you don't have a place to live.

Troy and his mother moved out when he was around five years old, to a subsidized housing development. While he had more friends in the projects, there was something about the farm that he missed. Grandma Wilhamenia was a big part of that. So was all the acreage on the farm; there might not have been a lot of toys to play with there, but with a little imagination, the possibilities were endless.

Some 15 to 20 years later, Troy would find himself in a football locker room and hear complaints from some of his teammates. Maybe practice went too long. Someone wanted a car, a tattoo, or a piece of jewelry. The body ached and maybe the paycheck wasn't big enough.

Those were the times when he would think back to Blackville and say to himself, "Every little crumb, every little thing, just appreciate it."

By the time he was 10, Grandma Wilhamenia moved out of the house on the farm, all of her kids now elsewhere. She couldn't do the work on the farm by herself.

That saddened the grandson. Time moves on. But the lessons learned on that farm would never fade.

* * *

Football was a big part of life in Blackville. High school football on Friday night, as it is in many places around the country with that *Friday Night Lights* mentality, was the local entertainment.

Troy was hooked on the game early, from the time he first began attending games with his aunt, who was in high school at the time. The local high school team was a perennial state title contender in the late '70s and into the early '80s, which further stoked his passions. Like many, he looked out on the field and said to himself, "Someday that will be me."

But that was still a few years away, so he played the more informal type football—in the projects with his friends. They'd play on the cornfields and every once in a while, kids from the projects from the other side of town would come by for an informal game, a grass-roots rivalry that Troy soaked up as if it were the Super Bowl. He was usually the youngest of the bunch. The smallest, too. But he had good hands and a knack for coming up with the tough catch, a scouting report that would follow him into the NFL.

A reminder that most of the people involved in the game were from modest backgrounds was reflected in the football itself. It was often tattered, the laces sometimes ripped. Occasionally, there would be a good ball, maybe even a tee to kick the ball, one that someone received as a present for Christmas or as a birthday gift. But that usually didn't last long.

If it wasn't football, it was baseball. That was another sport that didn't take much to get a game together among those in the country projects—some sticks, maybe some boards, and any old ball that might be around.

For kids growing up in the area, there weren't many options for organized sports—no little league soccer or pee-wee basketball. By the time Troy was old enough to try out for his first competitive bas-ketball team, in the seventh grade, he was cut from the middle-school squad. It would be the first hurdle for him to clear in a long athletic career of overcoming the odds.

He ended up playing competitive baseball for a few years, but the excitement he got from that paled in comparison to the way he felt when on the football field, or when he would watch a game, like he did that first time in Grandma Wilhamenia's bedroom/family room, when he saw the Dallas Cowboys and instantly fell in love with them.

So it was football. And more football. He had wanted to play organized football in the first grade, but was held back by family members concerned by his diminutive stature. So he'd follow his brother Dwayne to practice, a seven-year-old either walking the few miles or taking his bicycle and navigating little ditches in the road and getting chased by stray dogs at times.

There was naturally some fear in making those jaunts to practice, wondering if the boards that were set up to cover some ditches in the road would hold up. But he figured that if his older brother was going that way, he would do the same. If that meant being part of the action, he'd take the risk and attempt to conquer the fear.

So when the undersized first-grader arrived for his brother's first practice, he did what anyone would expect a seven-year-old to do—he negotiated. "Coach, put me in! I want to play! I want one of those uniforms!"

The coach said no. The boy cried.

The coach, perhaps feeling a bit beaten down, called the boy's mother to see if there was any wiggle room. But Troy's mom held her ground, like a nose tackle unwilling to be budged off the spot at the middle of the line of scrimmage.

The boy cried some more, until they found a solution that would work. Troy Brown would be the water boy.

It was perfect, really. An NFL player who would later be remembered as one of the most selfless teammates in New England Patriots history, not to mention one of its most clutch performers, just wanted to be part of the team.

It was that way in first grade. Just as it was that way when he was 37 in his final season in the NFL, having reached the mountaintop and chasing one more championship ring.

When Troy finally got his chance to play organized football the next season, there was a noticeable problem—the equipment didn't fit. Not even close.

His helmet looked like it could have fit two of his heads. His pants were falling down his waist, but that didn't really look so bad because his No. 22 jersey covered everything up as it extended down toward his knees.

"We'd tape his knee pads up, tape his thigh pads up around his waist, and the funny thing about his helmet is that when he would run, it would turn sideways on his head," recalled Al Sept, who coached the pee-wee team.

The first position Troy played was defensive back, which would help 25 years later when Bill Belichick put him there again.

Sept recalls that day in 1979 as if it were yesterday.

"I put Troy into the game and pointed to the wide receiver on the other team and said 'See that player? Everywhere he goes, I want you in his back pocket.' Troy said, 'Yes, sir.' So the teams get into their huddles and I'm making sure we have the correct number of players on our side, but we're short one player. That's because Troy was in the other team's huddle, in the back pocket of that wide receiver. He was doing exactly what I told him."

That required Sept to call a timeout and explain to Troy the rules of the game. These were the modest beginnings of Troy Brown, the future New England Patriots Hall of Famer.

Coach Sept also put him on the kickoff team, and in many ways, that was the highlight of his little league football career. Looking back, the synergy is hard to miss. When Brown's NFL career ended in 2007, he was known as one of the club's most clutch special teams players.

What little league coaches quickly discovered—just as Bill Parcells, Pete Carroll, and Bill Belichick later would in the NFL—was that while the little guy didn't always look great doing it, he simply made plays and never backed down from a confrontation. Maybe that's why he quickly graduated to playing offensive guard, defensive tackle, and running back.

One thing the coaches always told him, mainly because he was the smallest player on the field, was that he needed to protect himself from big hits. He never listened. There was a sense of pride he had in taking the big hit and getting back up, or dragging a few would-be tacklers along for a ride and later hearing them say, "He's pretty strong for a little dude."

"From Day 1, his drive to win and not give up stood out," recalled Coach Sept. "If his body was as big as his heart, you couldn't place him in a stadium. That's the type of individual Troy was at the time;

he was an exciting young man who loved what he did and knew the background he came from."

It's the same feeling he had when Bill Belichick said similar things to him in the Super Bowl championship years. While others looked at Troy as an undersized slot receiver, he viewed himself more in the mold of running back Antowain Smith, a 232-pound thumper who was known for running over defenders, not by them.

It was an approach that was born in the "country projects" of Blackville, when there were daily challenges between Troy's brother and his friends to see who held the title as the toughest of the bunch. At times, the group would coax little Troy to take part in what was essentially an "Oklahoma drill"—two players in confined space running full speed at one another, and may the toughest man (or in this case, boy) win.

Troy often won them. So while he might have been the smallest kid on the block, he never really felt like it. To prove his point, he'd often line up in the back row of team pictures, the spot normally reserved for the team's bigger players.

He always played big, of course.

When Troy would later become a New England Patriots fixture, he was one of the most famous athletes to ever come out of Blackville. Up to that point, running back Larry Raysor, who attended the University of Georgia, was probably the most well-known athlete from the town.

Troy has never forgotten those roots.

"Growing up with a single mother, having to work, seeing his mother struggle, Troy always wanted to make things better for his family; it was never just him, but also his mother, siblings, and his grandmother," said Sept, who has remained in close contact with Troy since those first pee-wee days.

"Troy didn't want his siblings to come up the way he did. He came up hard and it wasn't easy for him. He wanted to make sure he provided and that also includes giving back to the community.

"We had lost pee-wee football for 10 to 12 years, and when we decided to bring it back, I called Troy and asked for support. He dressed out 22 kids from top to bottom to make sure they had the same opportunity he did when he was a kid."

Such kindness helps explain why Troy once received the keys to the town.

"Troy put Blackville on the map," Sept said. "And in doing so, he was an example to kids of what can happen when you do the right things."

* * *

When Troy finally made it to the NFL, he quickly discovered how bringing in a new coach meant a dramatically different way of doing things. The transition from Bill Parcells to Pete Carroll was extreme in 1997. Then in 2000, the switch from Carroll to Bill Belichick also meant a dramatically different way of doing things.

It turns out it wasn't the first time he'd dealt with such change. In fact, a switch to a new coach when he was in 10th grade at Blackville-Hilda High School was the catalyst to his eventual breakthrough as a college prospect.

In his pee wee and middle school years, Troy played a lot of fullback and the team ran the power I-formation. It was an interesting fit considering he was one of the smallest players on the field, weighing 100 pounds as a freshman. The plays didn't vary much—run, run, and run some more.

That changed when Mike Pope became head coach in Troy's sophomore season, installing an offense that called more passing plays. An injury kept Troy out for most of that season, but by the time junior and senior year rolled around, and Troy had bulked up to about 130 pounds, he had transitioned to a full-time receiver.

"Eyes! Hands! Tuck!"

"Eyes! Hands! Tuck!"

"Eyes! Hands! Tuck!"

Those were the words the coaching staff constantly drilled into Troy and his fellow receivers and he took them to heart, going through each warm-up with intensity and learning the nuances of running different routes.

This, in many ways, was like a return to how he played in the country projects in Blackville. Troy wasn't known as a speed demon, but he was shifty and had reliable hands. Growing into his body, he flashed potential to be a difference-maker on teams that were about to break through to championship-contender status.

Senior year was special, a combination of his emergence and the presence of talented players around him to form a team that later would remind him of the 2001 New England Patriots Super Bowl championship squad because the "team" came before individual ego. Everyone just did their job and didn't care who got the credit, which was a bit different from his junior year. Blackville-Hilda High School lost just one game in Troy's senior season in 1989, finishing 14–1. The blemish coming when players were understandably distracted by the death of one of their teammates.

Inevitably, when former teammates meet up, they still reminisce about those days. What they often remember is what many do when they reflect mid-life: the innocence of it all, how they were led by their passion. When they took the field—and there were 5,000 to 10,000 people cheering them on, some lined up on the fence in back of the end zone—it felt like they meant something to everyone. No one was thinking about how hard life was at those times and that's the way it was supposed to be.

But life was hard, make no mistake about it.

Troy worked all the time, which is why football never really seemed like work to him. When he was nine years old, for example, he'd be picked up in the country projects in a station wagon and be driven to the cucumber fields. His responsibility was to fill five-gallon buckets full of cucumbers, and he'd earn 50 cents per bucket. That's a lot of cucumbers.

A tedious job to some, Troy took it seriously while making it a point to avoid the snakes slithering through the fields. He was meticulous, just as he was on the football field. If his route was supposed to be run at the six-yard mark, that didn't mean five-and-a-half yards or six-and-a-half yards. It was precisely six yards and picking the cucumbers was no different. It would have been easy to stock each bucket with big, old soggy cucumbers, but those wouldn't be appetizing for re-sale. So he had a process in which the smaller ones went into one bucket, the medium ones into another.

By day's end, it wasn't uncommon for 20 buckets to be filled and Troy to be walking off with $10. That was like striking it rich, and he'd often treat himself to some candy or soda pop as a reward. Not to mention, those buckets were huge, so it was a good workout too.

A few years later, Troy graduated from cucumbers to cantaloupes and made even more money. Some paid $30 to $40 per day. Others paid by the truckload, anywhere between $20 to $30, and it was common to see 18-wheelers and big dump trucks backing into the fields and Troy filling them up. The money was nice to have, helping to pay for his school clothes and also the family's electric bill, which was often significant because living in a single-wide metal trailer meant the air conditioner was always running in the summer months.

What Troy learned at such a young age is that you do what you have to do to support your family, and his eyes were always open for ways to make more money. At 15, he realized that while picking cucumbers had been lucrative, as had cantaloupes, there was even more money to be made with watermelons.

It was hot out there. And at times the smell of diesel fumes from the beaten-down trucks was so overwhelming it seemed like they were ripping through his body. But he persevered, awakening at 6:00 in the morning, getting to the fields, and joining a bunch of fellow workers to form what was essentially an assembly line. All the trucks were parked in rows, so the workers would line up across the road in front of them and pitch watermelons down the line to the truck.

Pick and pitch. Pick and pitch. Pick and pitch. The work was arduous and endless, but Troy took great pride in it, as he always did.

About 15 years later, in one of the unforgettable moments of his

NFL career, when he scooped up a blocked field goal in the 2001 AFC Championship Game against the Pittsburgh Steelers and lateraled to teammate Antwan Harris, it might as well have been a watermelon. He had done that so many times before.

He spent full days picking and pitching watermelons, and they ranged from 15 to about 55 pounds. A regular work day might have resulted in three full trucks being filled. As long as he avoided working for those who paid by the day, and instead paid by the watermelons themselves, the money was good. After a few weeks, he had pocketed anywhere from $500 to $600.

When the rotation called for it, Troy's job was to man the "bump" position, as he'd be on the side of the truck, which required him to touch every watermelon and get it onto the truck. He'd catch the watermelon, secure it, and then push it up.

"Pick and pitch" turned into "catch and push," and Troy felt that technique helped him as a football player. By picking and pitching, and then catching and pushing, he was using his legs to most effectively manage the weight of the watermelons. Maybe it would have been different if he was a little bigger, but he needed to maximize every part of his scrawny 100-pound body.

The work developed a toughness—both physical and mental—that would later serve him well in the NFL. With no tree cover and shade over the summer, the searing heat made it miserable at times, but workers had no choice but to wear long-sleeved shirts unless they wanted sunburns. This was Troy's summer job all through high school, and if there was an option for overtime with a Saturday delivery, he did that too. The money was too good to pass up. His family needed it.

This was the life that Troy knew, and if it meant picking peaches and pulling weeds out of the peanut fields (they wanted to clear as much pesticide out of the field as possible), that's what he did. It's why football and double-session Patriots training camp practices never really seemed like work to him. Those weren't even close to picking and pitching watermelons, and catching and pushing them into the truck.

When Troy's work was done each summer day, he'd often then head over to Blackville-Hilda and hit the weight room. The day would finish with maybe some pickup basketball.

All the while, his body was changing, muscles forming, and a maturity that belied his age was becoming ever so evident.

Sometimes he wonders how he got through those days. Mind over matter, he'd remind himself.

Troy watched his mother do that every day as the rock of the family. Her perseverance was remarkable. He had also seen how Grandma Wilhamenia was the glue that kept everything together in his early years on the farm.

The young boy was following in the footsteps of his role models, while at the same time carving out his own unique path.

Two

FROM JUNIOR COLLEGE TO MARSHALL, IMPROBABLY SO

So they did what recruiters often do, they
asked, "Who's the little guy?"

CHAPTER TWO

From Junior College to Marshall, Improbably So

Troy was the first in his family to attend college, earning a $500 scholarship to Lees-McRae Junior College in Banner Elk, North Carolina. For parts of his first year, he wondered why they gave him a scholarship at all because the coaches wouldn't play him.

Maybe it was because his fellow receivers were 6'3" and he was barely 5'8". When the buses left for road games, Troy was often left behind.

Kids who grew up in Blackville usually didn't go to college. Most of them worked in the local factories in town, making air conditioning and heating units, which is where Troy's mother and brother worked. Troy's brother also worked in a factory that produced soda machines and fan belts. Other kids went straight to the military.

So it wasn't like there were many examples for Troy to follow, to tell him that by going to college he'd give himself a chance at a better life.

Mike Pope, the football coach at Blackville-Hilda, opened his eyes to that possibility. Through his connections with coaches at Lees-McRae Junior College, several players had the opportunity to enroll there, including the team's top quarterback and running back.

That's one of the great parts about the game of football that can often be overlooked: Coaches who treat players like their own sons, looking out for them, giving them a chance at a better life than they've known. They teach values such as hard work and persistence and lead young men through the inevitable ups and downs of that challenging time in their lives.

Still, not everyone takes to the coaching, or seizes the chances provided. If ever there was an example that reflected that, it was the day Troy was signing his $500 scholarship.

Troy and his mother loaded up the car for the drive to Banner Elk, North Carolina, and headed on their way to pick up one of Troy's teammates, who was also set to sign a scholarship. They knocked on the door. There was no answer.

He wasn't coming, instead deciding to start his work life in the local factories.

In football, that would be known as the quarterback taking the check-down route, the safe play. Troy understood it, and there was a part of him that wanted to do the same thing because he didn't want to leave the comforts of home, even though life was never really comfortable, if that makes sense.

It cost about $7,500 to attend Lees-McRae at that time, so the $500 scholarship didn't cover much. Financial aid and grants helped offset some of the cost, and Troy and his mother scrounged together the rest. Troy once again picked up work in the fields, picking and pitching watermelons over the summer and cutting down Christmas trees in the fields behind where practice was held once football season ended.

The first semester at Lees-McRae was like a football game in which Troy's team fell behind early in the first quarter, and everything was a struggle because of it. He didn't take his studies seriously enough, often deciding that video games were a more effective use of his time than hitting his books. At times he would ask himself, "Why am I even here?"

He almost wasn't there after that first semester, teetering on the edge of flunking out and thinking about quitting the team.

Maybe it would have been different if he was actually playing football, but to him, it seemed as if the coaching staff had no use for him, the $500 scholarship apparently a case of charity. Even when he had good days at practice, and teammates acknowledged his fine work, it wasn't rewarded with playing time. Heck, he didn't even travel with the team to road games despite having what he felt were solid practices.

It took a few players getting hurt for Troy to finally get his chance, in a road game at Montgomery College in Rockville, Maryland. He crushed it, of course, scoring a couple of touchdowns and ringing up more than 100 yards receiving.

The coaches made sure to put him in the game after that.

Suddenly, the entire experience at Lees-McRae turned around for the better. Troy's scholarship increased from $500 his first year to $3,000. That was a big deal, not just for the finances, but also because it was a tangible reward for persevering through adversity.

It's not that Troy didn't know about hard times. His life had been full of them. But this was his shining example of how "It isn't where you start, it's where you finish."

How could he not think back to the day he signed that first scholarship? One of his teammates didn't even answer the knock at his door. Another had already decided not to attend.

Troy took the route less traveled, to a place he'd never heard of, and this was his reward. It was sweet, especially because he had been wrestling with the idea of giving it all up when things weren't initially going well.

It wouldn't be the first time he'd face adversity on the football field and overcome it. In fact, adversity was right around the corner.

* * *

Things were supposed to go better in Troy's second season at Lees-McRae Junior College, the result of his increased scholarship. But while he saw the value of his scholarship rise, his statistics dipped, in part because the offense was changing.

Troy had been through this before, but only in reverse. At Blackville-Hilda High School, he played in a run-based offense until new coach Mike Pope changed things his junior and senior seasons, opening up the passing game, which ultimately helped open the door to attend Lees-McRae.

With sagging statistics and a Lees-McRae team that wasn't as good as the year before, Troy wasn't exactly on the radar of college recruiters.

A few of his teammates, such as punter Travis Colquitt, were still getting attention and that turned out to be critical for him. This was a classic case of when college coaches come to see someone else—Miami, Florida State, Clemson, and Ole Miss had a regular presence at Lees-McRae that year—only to stumble on a scrappy player who would do anything just to be given a shot.

This is how then–Marshall University assistant coach Chris Scelfo first discovered Troy.

It was raining heavily and Scelfo was on campus to watch Lees-McRae practice, and everyone was accounted for except for an undersized, underdog receiver who was back in his dorm room sleeping. Troy's alarm never went off that day, as he had mistakenly set it for the wrong time, probably because he had been over-tired in the first place.

That can be the worst; the jarring feeling of knowing you'd just screwed up and cost yourself an opportunity to potentially further your career. It was so un-Troy, too. He had mostly been responsible throughout his life, in part because of the responsibility he took on to help his family financially.

Troy considered not even showing up for practice that day. It would be easier to run away from the problem than face it head on.

Then he considered manning up and laying it all out for the coaches—he had been exhausted, didn't set his alarm correctly, overslept, and felt terrible about the mistake.

It turns out he chose a different option, a Hail Mary type play, if you will. Troy ran as fast as he could to the athletic facilities—which meant following a narrow path and scaling a few inclines on the 10-minute journey—and showed up out of breath. He had planned to tell the coaches everything, except that when he arrived, nothing seemed out of the ordinary, so he simply tried to blend in as if he had been there all along.

Could this really work? Troy noticed Coach Scelfo and a few others in green Marshall University shirts standing in the corner of the gym, which is where the walkthrough practice was being held because of the rainy conditions, and when he arrived one of his coaches motioned to him to take his position on the makeshift field.

Troy couldn't believe it. He knew he should have been disciplined for a late arrival, but he was being given a break.

What he didn't realize is that another big break was also coming his way. Scelfo couldn't help but notice the moxie of the diminutive receiver who showed up late but was catching every football thrown in his direction. So they did what recruiters often do, they asked, "Who's the little guy?"

They received a glowing report about how Troy was one of the hardest workers on the team and would be an asset to any program— that is, assuming he showed up on time! That later turned out to be a bit of a running joke between Troy and Coach Scelfo, who remains one of his closest friends.

"We were down there and the team was working out in the gym that day because it was cold and wet," Scelfo recalled. "I saw this kid over there in the corner, playing catch with the cornerback, and he was small but every time the quarterback threw it you couldn't hear it hit his hands. We were waiting on the punter and I just kept watching this guy catching balls from the quarterback and he didn't drop anything. It was very smooth. We weren't looking for a receiver at the time but I asked the coach, 'Who is this over here? What's his background?' He told me he was a little undersized coming out, nobody recruited him, we got him, and he's been a big player for us."

At that point, Sclefo asked if it would be okay to speak with Troy. The request was granted, with Scelfo asking Troy if he had a highlight tape he could take back to Marshall.

"We had scheduled a visit with the punter to come up, and when I got back to look at the tape of Troy, I said, 'This guy can be an inside receiver for us.' We weren't really recruiting an inside receiver but in my mind this guy was good enough. So this was in late December and the first set of visits after that were in January. I asked our coach, Jim Donnan, saying, 'I really like this receiver.' He said he'd take a look at it, a couple coaches did, and nobody was jumping on the table for him."

So Sclefo did.

"I said, 'This guy right here can play! Can we bring him in?'"

But Donnan was firm in his stance. There were only so many scholarships to hand out, and an undersized, under-recruited slot receiver wasn't part of the plan.

Scelfo, however, was determined.

"We always had a recruiting meeting on Sunday, to go over where every coach was traveling, and who they were going to see," Scelfo recalled. "I said, 'Coach, can I bring Troy Brown in next weekend? There are only two weekends left to do this.' He said, 'Absolutely not! We don't have room for him.' We had a discussion for a little while and then we moved on."

Scelfo wasn't completely convinced, however. He had seen cases where scholarships open up at the last minute and he hoped one of those could be Troy's.

"The next weekend we brought guys in and it was the Sunday

before the last recruiting weekend. I said it again, 'Coach, I want to bring this guy in! Trust me on this one.'"

Donnan, perhaps a bit agitated at Scelfo's relentlessness, let his guard down and granted the visit for Troy. Scelfo was thrilled to make the phone call that day to Troy, relaying that the visit was for the upcoming weekend. Troy told him that he was ready, even though he had no idea how he'd get to the airport.

In those days, pre-email and iPhones, Troy was instructed by Scelfo to go to the airport and there would be a ticket waiting for him on Friday.

The whole turn of events was unforgettable to Troy because it was the first time he had ever been on an airplane. The quick hop from Johnson City, Tennessee, to Huntington, West Virginia, was on a propeller jet that bounced around like a bad spiral on a windy day, making his stomach queasy and leading him to curl up in his seat and bury his head between his legs. At one point, Troy tucked his return ticket into the pocket of the seat in front of him, a decision that would later lead to some angst. Remember, this was before the days of checking in for a flight over email and scanning boarding passes at the gate.

When he finally arrived for the visit, one thing struck Scelfo: it was cold and Troy wasn't wearing a jacket. Scelfo told him to wear his own Marshall jacket and he'd get it back at the end of the trip.

One of the first things that weekend was the recruiting dinner, which was a standard event where all the recruits attend and the staff gets to know them better. When Scelfo introduced Troy to the coaching staff, there was immediate resistance.

"Can't you see he doesn't fit here?"

"He's not tall enough!"

"How is he going to help us?"

"This is a waste of time!"

But Scelfo kept flashing back to what he saw in the gymnasium that day at Lees-McRae, the softness with which the ball hit Troy's hands, which was a culmination of years of practice, from the fields at Grandma Wilhamenia's farm to loading watermelons on the trucks to "Eyes! Hands! Tuck!" in high school. Then there was the explosiveness that Troy had shown on tape.

On those recruiting visits, prospective students usually spend a lot of time with other players, with each matched up with a specific host. Troy went out that Friday night and some of the players already on the team relayed to the coaching staff that Troy had made a positive impression...except for one small thing.

There was a pick-up type basketball game among them and Troy, never one to back down from competition, joined the game. It wasn't pretty and the way some players remember it, one player simply looked like he didn't belong, and it was Troy.

When word got to Donnan, the head coach, he was still wondering why Marshall was investing in a visit with Troy. He let Scelfo, who was championing Troy's cause along with recruiting coordinator Mark Gale, know that it sure seemed like this was a stretch.

Maybe it was a result of how relentless Scelfo was, or that the chips had fallen a certain way with other recruits, but Donnan ultimately softened. By the end of the weekend, he had made the decision that Troy would be offered a half-scholarship.

That alone was a major victory based on where the process had started. Yet Scelfo told Donnan that while it was a kind gesture, it wouldn't be accepted because Troy wasn't in position to pay the other half.

So Donnan called Troy in for a one-on-one meeting and that's when Troy started rattling off other schools who had reached out to him about possibly playing for them, knowing in the back of his mind that wasn't truly the case. It was Marshall...or who knows what he'd do?

Unlike a five-star recruit, Troy had to adopt the approach of salesman, telling Donnan why he was the right fit for them. He had no other schools knocking down his door and no great film to showcase his work, a result of the Lees-McRae offense sputtering his sophomore year.

Troy wasn't used to being put in the position of salesman, where gently twisting the truth to spark a deal getting done might be considered acceptable. If it meant telling Donnan that nearby Appalachian State and others had shown some interest in him, well, that just might have to be part of his sales pitch. The assistant coaches gave him assurances that approach would be acceptable.

So just as he often did on the football field, making the cornerback think he was running one route before breaking it off and executing another, Troy sold it hard.

Appalachian State...East Tennessee State...Western Carolina... Tennessee-Chattanooga. He started rattling off schools that had "shown interest," hoping that Donnan would see that one of his precious few scholarships remaining would be well-used on him.

Then came an excruciating wait, with Donnan telling him to hang loose outside his office as he called his assistants in for a chat. It seemed like hours, with Troy going through all the possibilities in his head. He would take anything—partial scholarship, a few bucks here or there, anything to be given a shot.

Then Donnan called him in and said, "You know what, son? I think I'm going to scrounge up an extra scholarship, and give it to you."

Troy was stunned. Pleasantly so, considering he wasn't even sure he would be able to get a ride to the airport that day. He didn't have a car at junior college and had always resisted asking others for favors. So it wasn't until the day of his trip, which few of his teammates knew about in the first place, that he finally stepped out of his comfort zone and asked one of his pals for a ride.

No, it wasn't the perfectly executed game plan. But sometimes the hurry-up offense works, too.

This is all part of the great underdog story of Troy Brown, who didn't even have gas money to give his teammate that day for the 45-minute drive. He cut it so close, in fact, that he almost missed the flight altogether, which reflected how he was just getting by, chasing a dream but without the road map many others had.

This wasn't the linebacker and defensive back that Ole Miss had come to recruit. This wasn't the lineman who had his ticket punched to go to Clemson. This wasn't the receiver who went to Northeast Louisiana to team up with Vincent Brisby, who would later become Troy's teammate with the Patriots.

All those highly touted players had come to Lees-McRae with

a plan—improve their grades and then they would play Division I football. It was a pitstop.

For Troy, Lees-McRae was more likely to be the end game. And even then, it would have been a victory, because he knew all too well what he was leaving behind.

Many of his friends from high school were back in Blackville, getting caught up in the wrong things—too many drugs, too much alcohol. Others worked in the factories, making grills, fan belts, and other stuff, or they just went to the military.

By blazing his own trail, and putting himself out of his comfort zone by accepting the $500 scholarship, Troy saw an "out" route.

The next route he would run would be for Marshall. Simply amazing, and he'd forever be indebted to Scelfo for opening that door for him.

There was only one small issue remaining: How would Troy get back to Lees-McRae after his recruiting visit?

* * *

Chris Scelfo couldn't believe it.

The hardest part of all, which was getting Troy a scholarship to Marshall, had been achieved. Scelfo had heard good things from players already on the team about how Troy would fit in, as he had earned their immediate respect on the recruiting weekend. So Scelfo was already starting to think about ways in which he and the coaching staff could put Troy in a position where his athleticism could shine, and wanted to ensure Troy's mother, Richadean, that Troy would be well taken care of.

"We were in the car heading back to the airport, he was all excited and I was excited because I really thought he could help us," Scelfo recalled. "So we get there and he didn't have his dang ticket!"

In those days, there was no iPhone app or Twitter direct message to rectify the problem. It was a paper ticket and Troy figured he'd mistakenly left it on the plane en route to Marshall.

At that point, Scelfo had a few options to consider. He could call Marshall coach Jim Donnan and see if he would sign off on the $247 charge for a new ticket. Or he could try Plan B.

"I sure wasn't going to call Coach Donnan!" Scelfo joked. "So I called my wife to ask her if we had enough credit on our credit card to be able to charge this one-way ticket. She looked it up and told me, 'Yeah, you can charge it, but we really don't have any more money after that.' So I paid for his ticket, put him on the plane, and he took my jacket too!"

Scelfo and Troy still laugh about that one. And given their struggle to secure the scholarship, they ultimately got the last laugh as Troy starred at Marshall for two years, breaking numerous school records and turning Donnan into one of his biggest boosters.

But as one would expect given his situation, Troy had to bide his time before breaking through. He was referred to as "Transcript" by coaches.

Mark Gale, Marshall's recruiting coordinator, laughed when telling the story of how the "Transcript" nickname was born.

"It was August and we were sending all the players' transcripts in to the admissions office, and there was an issue with Troy; they discovered at the last moment he had taken a summer school course at Voorhees College in South Carolina. I called Troy and said we had to have a transcript of every school he had attended, and we didn't have that one.

"Then we called Voorhees and they told us they were in the middle of registration and it might be a while before they could get it for us. So I said, 'What if I pick it up? Could it be ready?' They said it could.

"We had a booster with a single-engine prop plane who let us use it in emergency situations, and we were running out of time getting Troy's transcript. So here I am, on a half-dirt/half-grass runway, getting on this small plane to go to Voorhees. I got the transcript and made it back with about 15 to 20 minutes to spare."

Later, Troy would repay the favor to Gale by sending him an autographed New England Patriots picture with the words, "Thanks for flying 400 miles to make me a part of the greatest team I've ever played on."

If Scelfo had been Troy's No. 1 backer from a recruiting standpoint, Gale quickly became a believer. He recalled the first time he watched Troy—initially traveling to Murfreesboro, Tennessee, for a junior college all-star game that was actually being played in Murfreesboro, North Carolina.

"He stood out, but for some reason other schools didn't see it," Gale said. "If you measured him height-wise, just eye-balling him, he didn't pass the test. But what you can't measure is his heart.

Talk about a competitor.

"I'll never forget when he showed up for his first day at Marshall, he had a green Army duffle bag. In it was everything he owned."

That also stood out to Marshall teammate Ricardo Clark, who

had hosted Troy on his recruiting visit and offered to drive Troy to campus for the start of training. When they met in the parking lot of a local mall, Troy had the one bag.

"I said to him, 'You do realize you're going to school?'" Clark recalled. "When you think about that, it is a reminder that he did so well for himself coming from humble beginnings."

On that car ride to Marshall, Clark estimates that Troy might have said a total of seven words. He was shy.

Soon enough, the two became the closest of friends and Troy— often times playing video games like *Joe Montana Football* and *Bill Walsh College Football* with teammates—would loosen up.

"Once he got comfortable, you couldn't get him to stop talking," said Clark, who was later in Troy's wedding and remains one of his closest pals. "He became one of the pranksters on the team, cracking jokes. But he always remembered where he came from. His mom, family, and friends were the most important thing to him."

Football was up there, too, and Troy quickly made Coach Scelfo look good by performing well.

"Then when he got on the field, the bottom line was that he had a chip on his shoulder. He knew he was a step slow, a couple inches short, but you could see his determination and that he wanted to be successful.

"Did anybody, myself included, and him too, see the success he would have in football? I don't think so. But was he going to be successful in life? Absolutely, positively. It just so happened to be football. But I saw that from the initial meeting we had. You knew he was going to be somebody."

Troy ultimately transitioned from "Transcript" to pure playmaker, often making plays when he touched the ball, either as a return man or a receiver.

His first foray into the world of the return man was unexpected.

Even when a football game gets lopsided and many of the fans have already headed to the exits or turned the channel on their television, important things can happen to shape the future of a player, and such was the case with Troy in his first year at Marshall.

Morehead State, the alma mater of former New York Giants quarterback and current CBS football analyst Phil Simms, was losing to Marshall when Troy was on the sideline and heard the following: "Go back there and return the punt!"

His first instinct was: "Are you serious?"

Troy hadn't been extensively practicing punt returning, and it wasn't like he particularly enjoyed doing it, following the trajectory of the ball through the air, trying to catch it, while at the same time feeling the pressure of 11 players on the opposing team sprinting down the field in hopes of delivering a big hit.

In some ways, this was like his first experience with football as a kid, playing on the cornfields. Some people call special teams "organized chaos," and that's the way it was growing up—if you had the ball, you had to prepare to be hit hard.

Troy delivered one of the few highlights that day vs Morehead State—a punt return for a touchdown.

This was good and bad, of course. The good part was that Troy, as always, would do anything possible to help his team score points and win a game. The bad? Well, he was going to be fielding a lot more punts in the coming weeks, taking his close friend Ricardo Clark's job in the process, the same friend he lived with over the summer while training for the season.

Troy was good at it. Really good. In 1991, he wound up leading Division I-AA in punt return average, as well as kickoff return average, emerging as one of the nation's most dynamic return men, his 29.69 yard kickoff return average was a college football record that has stood for more than two decades. "If you put the ball in his hands, you knew there was a chance of him going all the way," Clark said.

Much like the punt returning job, the kickoff return duties were given to him on a whim and, in a familiar script, he returned one of his first attempts for a touchdown.

The next season, Marshall won a national championship and Troy wasn't just their top-flight returner, he was also a go-to receiver for Jim Donnan's team. A play at the end of the national championship foreshadowed Troy's NFL career, when he was put on the field to help defend a Hail Mary pass and came away with an interception.

Special teams...offense...defense. Troy did it all, which Patriots fans would later learn was simply the "Troy Brown way."

"If you [got] the ball in his hands, he was electrifying," said Phil Ratliff, a former teammate who is currently coaching at the University of North Carolina-Charlotte. "We knew by getting him involved on offense, he could change the outcome of a game. That was also true on special teams, and even when we put him on defense; him coming away with that ball at the end of the national championship was one of the biggest plays I remember from his career."

Troy had played the nickel cornerback in that national championship game, once again foreshadowing what he'd later do for the Patriots in the 2004 Super Bowl season.

If there is a lesson to be learned, it's that Troy always put himself in position to take advantage of any opportunity that came his way, which was the way it was in little league, high school, and junior college, too. This wasn't a five-star recruit who had a starting job handed to him. He had to earn everything, knowing his margin for error wasn't as great as other teammates.

This meant overcoming some fear, because to this day, he has always had some trepidation over fielding punts. He loved pretty much everything about football…except punt returning.

The idea that he might drop one kept him up at night. The feeling of 11 players on the opposing team building up a head of steam and attempting to knock his head off wasn't too comforting either. There was a lot to think about as that ball was in the air.

Kickoffs were much different. If he dropped the football on a kickoff, there was usually time to pick it back up and still make a play. Punt returns are much more of a bang-bang play—drop it, and the other team has a very good chance of recovering.

So Troy figured something out on the fly. If he caught the punt while moving forward, it increased his comfort level. Ultimately, his return skills helped lead him to the NFL.

Marshall's success as a team helped, too, because scouts had good reason to come to Huntington. In Troy's first season, Marshall lost to Jim Tressel's Youngstown State team in the national championship, an early lead squandered as the Thundering Herd faded late. One of Troy's fondest memories of that season was the bond he developed with teammates, which later reminded him of the tight-knit group from his Patriots days.

To Troy, that team was a bunch of scrappers, undersized from a height-weight perspective, but battle-tested players who thrived in clutch situations. That served as a lesson to Troy that would serve him well as his professional career unfolded—it's nice to have size, but it takes much more than that to succeed.

Marshall won the national championship the following season. Troy was putting up big numbers, and he was dreaming of the NFL; he averaged a touchdown for every eight times he touched the ball. Then he was crushed by not receiving an invite to the Combine, the annual event which brings most of the top college prospects together in Indianapolis so NFL teams can interview them, give them physicals, and learn more about them.

That hurt more than a big hit on a punt return. *How could they overlook me?*

Luck and timing play a big part in determining who is successful in football and Troy had seen this play out with some of his Marshall teammates before. They were some of the most talented players he had ever played with, yet they also were overlooked by the NFL, probably as a result of playing at a smaller college where the size of offensive and defensive linemen was the biggest difference between Division I-AA competition and upper-echelon Division I schools.

"That was something we would discuss a lot early in his career," said Will Brown, a teammate and close friend at Marshall. "He would say, 'Will, all the guys at Michigan and big schools, they aren't better than us.' He was adamant about that. He felt we just needed a break to show what we could do."

Troy took the Combine snub as a shot at him personally. He was furious. Yes, even someone like Troy, with a laid-back personality, can get fired up. He wasn't the type of player who was into self-promotion, or was a big talker to the media, touting his own accomplishments, but he was also proud of what he had accomplished. It made little sense to him that college football's most productive returner wasn't at the Combine, not to mention part of the Kodak All-American team.

Just as his future teammate, New England Patriots quarterback Tom Brady, has long kept a chip on his shoulder from being a sixth-round draft choice in 2000—the 199th overall selection—this was Brown's main motivation.

No one thought he was good enough. To this day, it still bothers him that another receiver from Division I-AA, Kenny Shedd of Northern Iowa, was invited to the Combine over him.

Troy later heard that part of the reason he wasn't invited was because the NFL draft was being trimmed from 12 rounds to eight, so there was a limit on how many players could attend. Others told him that he didn't run well at his Pro Day—when scouts come to campus for the purpose of putting prospects through a variety of drills—and that was part of it, too.

"But what about the production?" he thought to himself.

Troy wasn't about to stop dreaming of the NFL, and he later learned that a connection between Marshall coach Jim Donnan and first-year Patriots coach Bill Parcells was the key to him getting his shot to play professionally. Donnan, who had initially resisted recruiting Troy but who had quickly become a believer, reached out to Parcells and told him that Brown was his type of guy. To be a "Parcells guy" meant something, although that wasn't something Troy fully understood at the time.

By the eighth round of the NFL draft in April of 1993, Troy's phone rang and Parcells was on the other line. They exchanged a quick hello, and Parcells informed Brown he was the team's eighth-round draft pick (198th overall), before he said, "Thanks Troy, you just saved me a lot of money."

It was classic Parcells.

The Patriots possibly would have had to pay Brown a bit more had they signed him as an undrafted free agent—when other teams could have upped the bidding price—but a $15,000 signing bonus was chump change to an NFL team at the time. That's what Brown received in his first contract.

But this wasn't about money. This was about chasing an NFL dream that he'd thought of since his days living on Grandma Wilhamenia's farm.

Troy Brown was heading to the NFL, against all odds.

Three

THE NFL DREAM
ALMOST DIES

"Troy," Parcells said, "you'll never be a starting receiver in this league. Just a role player is the ceiling for you. Maybe a fourth or fifth receiver is the best you can do."

CHAPTER THREE

The NFL Dream Almost Dies

Bill Parcells is a Pro Football Hall of Famer, one of the greatest coaches of all-time, and historically hardest on the players he liked the most.

Troy was a "Parcells guy" and he could never forget one of his first meetings with him.

"Troy," Parcells said, "you'll never be a starting receiver in this league. Just a role player is the ceiling for you. Maybe a fourth or fifth receiver is the best you can do."

Excuse me, sir? This wasn't exactly what Troy had hoped to hear now that his NFL dream had been realized. He also looked around and saw players he felt he could compete with, even if he was coming from a smaller-school background.

But what Troy quickly came to realize was that this was how Parcells got the best out of his players. He poked and prodded them. He didn't sugarcoat things in the least.

What soon developed was an affectionate bond between player and coach. Troy loved Parcells, first for giving him an opportunity, and second for never having to wonder where he was coming from.

While playing for a coach like that might seem difficult for those looking from the outside, it was the approach Troy himself preferred.

Give it to me straight. Let me know what I have to do. And let's get to work.

In 1993, the Patriots as a franchise were in many ways reflective of Troy's own career—at the bottom of the barrel and hoping to claw their way back up. Parcells was hired and restored immediate credibility based on this track record and Super Bowl pedigree with the New York Giants.

The first training-camp practice was unforgettable. Those were the days when the team trained at Bryant University in Smithfield, Rhode Island (then called Bryant College), and a routine day was to have double-session workouts—the first at 8:15 in the morning, and then another in the scorching afternoon heat.

Players were in full pads that first morning, which would never happen these days, and the hitting was intense. After stretching and warmups, the first full-team drill included pad-crunching hits and veteran defensive back Adrian White was part of a big-time collision that caught everyone's attention, maybe no one more than Troy himself.

White, who had entered the NFL as a highly touted second-round pick of the Giants in 1987—another "Parcells guy" if you will—was one of the bigger defensive backs at the time at about 6' and 200 pounds. He towered over Troy and this was a tone-setting play on the first practice of training camp—a catch over the middle and...*Bam!*

Troy was thankfully watching on the sideline because he wasn't part of the first-unit at the time. Remember, Parcells told him that would never happen.

Troy's first thought: "Whoa! This NFL stuff is for real!"

Hits like that didn't happen at Lees-McRae or Marshall unless it was an accident, but this was the NFL life that Troy hoped to thrive in, even as his coach reminded him he might not be around for too long. It was almost as if Parcells himself had scripted it. He was the master manipulator, after all.

What Troy never told Parcells was that he was actually a big fan of his, having followed him closely while a student at Blackville-Hilda High School. Like many others, it was hard not to notice champions, and Parcells' Giants teams were a perennial Super Bowl contender. Pictures of Parcells being carried on the shoulders of players after championships weren't hard to find.

So while he didn't agree with Parcells' assessment of his skills, he respected it. It became his goal to prove Parcells wrong, which of course, is exactly how Parcells wanted it.

In time, Troy realized there was a soft side of sorts behind the gruff exterior of the Super Bowl–winning coach. Yes, he yelled at this players. A lot. But players also saw a different side of him.

Some of Troy's favorite memories as a football player were those that took place behind the scenes, in the locker room with teammates like Keith Byars, Sam Gash, Curtis Martin, and Shawn Jefferson as they played dominoes, chess, or Scrabble, and Parcells would mingle by and join them. The discussion often wasn't about football.

"Are you guys paying your taxes?"

"How many cars do you have? I hope not too many."

"Let me see what kind of jewelry you have on."

The environment Parcells created was one where some players, like Troy, felt as if he was taking an interest in them as people as much as players. Sometimes he offered financial advice.

"Don't you guys be buying any horses. You have to feed them. You won't make any money unless you win and it's hard to win."

Parcells, of course, was a big fan of the racetrack. Still is.

For Troy, that caring presence meant a lot when considering the modest background in which he grew up. He listened closely when Parcells told stories about how he'd hired some of his former players on his coaching staff, helping them get their finances in order when others had stolen from them, or they made some bad financial decisions themselves. Pacells was always careful not to disclose names.

That took away some of the sting when Parcells decided to rip into him, or the team.

That happened often, with quarterback Drew Bledsoe a frequent target. That was different for Troy to see, because every team he'd been part of, the quarterback usually was spared such wrath. In this case, Parcells treated Bledsoe like an undrafted free agent.

Like the times Bledsoe would throw a high pass in practice, Parcells asked him why it seemed like every pass he was throwing was intended for Shawn Bradley, who was a 7'6" center in the NBA at the time, not a member of the Patriots.

Bledsoe privately seethed, while teammates like Troy said to themselves, "If he's talking that way to the quarterback, imagine what he'd say to me."

"Hey Drew," Parcells would bark out. "How come every time our receivers have to make a catch, it has to be the National League Catch of the Week?"

Troy wasn't spared from the wrath.

"Brown!" Parcells would yell. "Get your pads down or you're going to be going home in a box. A very small box!"

Usually the players simply absorbed the verbal assaults, but there was one time it almost escalated into some notable fireworks.

Offensive lineman Pat Harlow, a first-round draft choice from 1991 under then-coach Dick MacPherson, had been poked in the eye during practice and Parcells might not have seen what happened when he starting ripping into him. Harlow fired back at him, threatening to come after him.

Well, Parcells didn't back down. He said he had something left in him and he was saving it for Harlow. Nothing happened, but that was one time where players like Troy wondered if maybe the prodding was going to escalate into something bigger. "I got one good fight left in me. Golden Gloves," Parcells said.

That was simply Parcells' coaching style; he was on players all the time. Even running back Curtis Martin, who later picked Parcells as his Hall of Fame presenter, was nicknamed "Boy Wonder" or "The One-Game Wonder." Martin was widely respected in the locker room, and that one hit home with Troy because the two would often play Scrabble and chess together.

So Parcells was consistent—he got on everyone, from the quarterback to the top running back to the eighth-round draft pick. When players didn't show up in shape for the conditioning test to start the year, Parcells would remind them, "If I can't get rid of your butt, then I'll run your butt until you do pass it!"

Troy viewed Parcells as a character, a lively presence that added a spark at practice and entertained the crowd as well who also had a softer side that he showed behind the scenes. This made him a complex coach to play for, but one thing was crystal clear to Troy: Parcells was about bottom-line results, and Troy learned that the hard way when he thought his NFL dream might officially be over.

*　*　*

By 2008, when Troy officially retired and became one of the all-time most popular Patriots, affection for him grew so great because everyone saw how his career almost never got started.

The defining moment came in the 1994 preseason finale at Green Bay.

As an eighth-round draft choice, Troy didn't have the same margin for error as other players, such as quarterback Drew Bledsoe, the No. 1 overall draft pick in his 1993 class. Troy had been one of the team's primary punt returners as a rookie, with 25 attempts for 224 yards (9.0 avg.) and nine fair catches. He also chipped in as a kickoff returner, with 15 runbacks for 243 yards (16.2 avg.), to go along with two catches for 22 yards.

Not exactly eye-popping stuff, so as the '94 preseason was coming to a close, he had an itch to make something happen to solidify his place on the roster. Opportunities to that point of the preseason had been sparse.

Then he fumbled the ball away against the Packers, a result of trying to do too much. He can recall the play vividly—what seemed like a wall in front of him, the hope that maybe an opening would present itself, and a voice in his head saying, "Somebody block someone, please!"

There was nothing there and he should have just gone down. In football, that's also called "live to get to the next play." But instead, Troy had a momentary lapse of concentration, standing upright and allowing the football to be ripped from his grasp.

No, not again. This opened an old wound, as he had lost a fumble in the home opener against Detroit as a rookie when an opponent surprised him by slipping the would-be blocking attempt of teammate Chris Slade and delivering a bone-crunching blow that separated him from the football with violent force. Then-Lions safety Willie Clay, who would later become a teammate, scooped up the ball and raced for an early-game touchdown.

One could argue that play wasn't necessarily Troy's fault. Slade's block wasn't very good and the hit was similar to what Troy had seen on the first day of training camp with Adrian White—a striking blow that probably would have produced the same result regardless of if it was a rookie or veteran as the returner.

But the fumble in the preseason against the Packers (in 1994) was different. Troy just had the ball taken from him, which left Parcells no choice but to take his job from him.

He was cut the next day.

Maybe Parcells was right, that Troy didn't have it in him to be a front-line contributor for a team. It wasn't like others were knocking down his door looking to pick him up, either.

So Troy packed up his things, returned home, and kept himself in shape, hoping that this wouldn't be the end of his NFL career.

He had resisted getting a job because he wanted to be ready for the possibility of an NFL team calling, but after a few weeks, his hopes started to diminish. He began working at the local Boys & Girls Club, also making plans to return to school to complete his degree.

So disappointed with the turn of events, he even started scaling back his workouts, losing the one thing that always seemed to fuel him from the early days on Grandma Wilhamenia's farm, to high school, junior college, and Marshall—hope.

The NFL dream was indeed fading.

"When he got released, he was crushed, his family was crushed, and we all felt it," recalled his close friend Ricardo Clark.

The Patriots were seven games into their 1994 season and Troy figured he was all but forgotten. He still watched games on television because he had friends on the team and it pained him to see one of his good friends, Ronnie Harris, make the same mistake he did. The Patriots were playing on the road against Pete Carroll's New York Jets when Harris fumbled a punt at the 38-yard line that the Jets ultimately turned into a touchdown with just less than two minutes remaining in the first half.

Troy wondered if his phone might ring, and sure enough, it did. One of the team's top personnel executives, Bobby Grier, was on the other end of the line.

"Troy, we need you back first thing in the morning. Get to the airport to pick up your tickets."

He could hardly sleep that night. When something gets taken away from you that you've been working so hard for, and you're not sure it will ever come back, there is a greater appreciation for it when it does.

This is one of the great lessons of Troy's NFL journey—to succeed, he first had to fail.

It led to introspection that paved the way for a career that would ultimately result in Troy's induction to the team's Hall of Fame.

When he returned to Foxborough, Massachusetts, he made a promise to himself: If he was to ever be cut again, it would never, ever, ever be for a lack of effort or a breakdown in concentration. He had to maintain his edge at all times.

One of the things he had a lot of time to think about was how he had approached his second preseason with the Patriots, in 1994. He had become slightly arrogant, thinking he had arrived. He started believing his press clippings, showing up on Marshall's campus in the off-season and allowing himself to believe he was the big man on campus, even cutting some of his workouts short at times.

But that's the thing about the NFL, especially for those taking an underdog path like Troy—you never really arrive. This game is simply too fragile, too violent, too humbling, to think you've got it all figured out. It took getting cut and spending long days in South Carolina and back at Marshall for Troy to realize this.

He knew he was better than he had showed in the 1994 preseason. In fact, he didn't blame Parcells for cutting him because he would have done the same thing had he been the coach. A player just had a ball taken from him? Unacceptable.

So the Patriots saw a different Troy Brown in his second stint with the team. He was a humbled player.

The dream was back on and he was determined to stick around this time, which meant no one was going to outwork him, and he would never, ever take a play off.

In that sense, this was like a return to his roots. He was going to approach each day as if he was loading watermelons onto the diesel-fumed trucks, just like he did as a youngster.

* * *

Just as Troy was approaching his career with a newfound determination, the Patriots were attempting to make a U-turn of their own. Troy's rookie season in 1993, as well as the 1994 season in which he received the second chance that he didn't know would ever come, were defining times in franchise history.

As they often say in the NFL, the tone is set at the top, and when Troy was drafted, James Orthwein was the team's owner. Not that Troy really knew much about him. He hardly saw him. The only time he did was on the day he sold the team to Robert Kraft in January of 1994.

One of the first things Troy noticed when Kraft took charge was his presence. Having the owner around the team was a much different feel from the prior year, and he could feel the change from the first time Kraft addressed the team as a whole. One of the things Troy liked to do during training camp at Bryant University was feed fish in the main pond on campus, and sometimes Kraft and his wife, Myra, would join him. They struck up a casual conversation, and Troy became Myra's favorite player.

Later, Kraft would tell the story about how Troy helped smash the stereotype that his late wife might have had of football players at the time. Kraft had committed $172 million of family resources to purchase the team, and was questioned by Myra about the intelligence of that decision.

Troy, it turned out, helped change that perception.

While the ownership change created a different vibe around the team, one thing remained the same: subpar facilities.

Not that Troy was really in any position to judge it all. He was just happy to be there.

But the Foxboro Stadium natural grass playing field was usually voted 28th out of the 28 teams when players took part in a survey to judge the quality and safety of the field. The only time that changed was in 1995 when expansion teams Carolina and Jacksonville joined the NFL. Then the Patriots usually dipped to 30th.

What Troy remembers most is that when he walked out on the playing field, he never really knew what he was going to get that day. It could be muddy. Maybe another day it would be more like playing on dirt. Other times, it was almost like driving over a road filled with potholes, the divots in the field creating a hazard for sprained ankles.

In time, Troy actually grew to appreciate it because in a sense, it was like playing on the farm at Grandma Wilhamenia's in Blackville, South Carolina. It had a real throwback, old-school type feel, fitting him well.

As for the locker room, well, that was another story. Troy would think to himself, "Hey, this is the NFL; there shouldn't be a situation where players don't have any hot water in the shower after a game." The showers and locker room were directly next to the opponents' and usually they could hear the team they had just played through the walls. It was that modest.

There were steel benches in front of each locker stall, and those weren't very pleasant to sit on either. A simple cushion would have been nice, but players looking for those types of extras were usually left disappointed. One time, Troy remembers asking for a new jock strap and was told he couldn't have it. So he took the old, gray, beat-up pair of socks that had been handed to him and returned to the steel bench in front of his locker, shaking his head.

When Troy was chasing his NFL dream, he envisioned a life of luxury, not this. He'd sometimes ask veteran players if it was like this everywhere, and in some cases, it apparently was. He had only seen one other facility, the Bengals' stadium, during a visit there before the 1993 NFL Draft. That didn't wow him either.

Troy describes that chapter in his time with the Patriots as "pre-Kraft" and "rough and rugged." Things began to change in the ensuing years and it later gave Troy an appreciation for when the team's state-of-the-art facility, Gillette Stadium, was built in 2002.

Some might say the subpar facilities strengthened the bond among players, sparking them to band together in an underdog, blue-collar manner. But that might be overstating it. To Troy, what stood out more than anything else was the quality of his teammates as people, and that they were good football players, too.

One player who Troy felt embodied that as much as anyone was fullback Sam Gash.

By nature of the position, Gash wasn't going to garner big head-lines, but he carried himself in a way that made it easy to follow him—from his hard-hitting style on the field to the classy boots he used to wear on road trips. Troy often played dominoes and Scrabble with Gash, and learned quickly that if he was ever in a time of need, Gash was someone to turn to.

If Gash was one of the leaders among players, there was no question who was the "Big Tuna" of the franchise. It was Parcells and his presence created a buzz in the region which Troy couldn't help but notice during his first training camp in 1993.

The Patriots were 2–14 the year before, but the crowds were now overflowing at camp, with many coming to see Parcells and the new hot-shot quarterback selected with the No. 1 overall pick, Drew Bledsoe. Expectations were higher than one might expect, but things didn't get off to a great start, with the team going 1–11 to open that year.

What stood out to Troy wasn't the record as much as how the Patriots were losing those games. So many of them were close: a 19–16 loss to the Lions in Week 2, when his own fumble put the team in an early hole; two losses to the Seahawks by a combined four points; losing to the Colts and Bills by a field goal in each game.

They were close, but just needed to find a way to get over that proverbial hump. By finishing out the year with four straight victories to post a 5–11 record, there was optimism for what was to come.

Then when the Patriots opened the following year with a 3–2 record, that optimism peaked that much more. Of course, Troy wasn't around for those games. That was the stretch when he was back home, a result of that costly fumble in the preseason finale at Green Bay, wondering if he'd ever play in the NFL again.

But as things dipped for the Patriots—they dropped games to

the Raiders, Jets, Dolphins, and Browns—the door opened for Troy because of Ronnie Harris' fumble in the Jets game. Troy's first two games back with the Patriots were losses, the second of which came against Bill Belichick's Cleveland team.

The Patriots were 3–6 when the Vikings came to town and built a 20–0 lead late in the second quarter. This is the game that Troy points to that officially turned Patriots football around, when the team finally learned how to win.

Foregoing the running game, Parcells put the game in Bledsoe's hands and the results were electric. Bledsoe ended up throwing 70 times, and the Patriots roared back to win in overtime 26–20.

Troy was used solely as the punt returner in the game, finishing with three returns for 24 yards, as he wasn't yet a big part of the offensive attack. However, he vividly remembers two things from that day—fullback Kevin Turner catching the game-winning 14-yard touchdown pass in the corner of the end zone, which led Foxboro Stadium to erupt, and the feeling in the locker room afterward among players that they had just had a breakthrough.

The Patriots won their final seven regular-season games that year, the ride coming to an end in a road playoff loss to Belichick's Browns team. Troy didn't have a reception all season, but led the team with 24 punt returns for 202 yards (8.4 average), with a long of 38 yards. Not exactly off-the-charts statistics.

While he felt a bit more secure with his place on the roster, he knew that he was still one mistake away from possibly being out of a job, so when he occasionally had entered the game as a receiver, there were plenty of nerves. In those years, being a No. 4 receiver meant you saw maybe a handful of snaps each game, usually on third down, which is much different than today's spread-it-out-and-throw-it NFL. Houston, with its run-and-shoot offense, was the one exception.

So the way it usually worked was that on third down, the Patriots would take their fullback, Sam Gash, off the field and replace him with either another fullback or a tight end that maybe had some more pass-catching skills.

Because of this, Troy didn't receive many repetitions in practice—he was behind Michael Timpson, Vincent Brisby, and Ray Crittenden on the depth chart—and he had to be patient in hopes that his opportunity might one day come. Sometimes he'd substitute in as a third-down running back, which was the coaches' way of trying to get the ball into his hands, but there was only one problem: that also required he block big, physical pass-rushers at times and it didn't work out so well for him. Parcells saw Troy splattered on the ground a few times and pulled the plug on that experiment.

Such a situation is one that many NFL players struggle with because they had been front-line players in college and high school.

Looking back, the simplistic nature is what stands out to Troy. When he did take the field, a simple play-call was "Six, Eighty-two, Curl," which in many ways was the extent of the team's third-down package. Later in his career, as the team's system grew from coordinator Ray Perkins to Charlie Weis and Josh McDaniels, the verbiage would become much more expansive.

Of course, at that point, Troy didn't know how long he'd be in the NFL, doubting that the team's own receivers coach, Chris

Palmer, thought he had what it took to play in the league. One discussion between the two stood out and it was when Palmer suggested that perhaps Troy was a better fit in the Canadian Football League because the field was wider and longer. Ouch.

So when Troy arrived for training camp in 1995, any security he felt about his roster spot was pretty much gone: "If my own coach thinks I am a CFL-caliber player, I'm probably not sticking around here too long."

Then something clicked in the 1995 preseason.

That's the funny part about being a backup receiver, you sort of develop a connection with the backup quarterback and your hopes are almost tied together. So it was for Troy and Scott Zolak, living life on the fringes of the roster, as they hooked up for some notable plays as the team played four preseason games—at home against Detroit and Minnesota, and on the road at Philadelphia and Oakland.

"I'd feed him," Zolak remembered, saying the connection between the two started in practice.

In those days, Zolak and Troy were part of the scout team and Zolak would irritate Parcells by not following instructions.

"They would always diagram the plays and circle where to throw it. But wherever they circled to throw it, that guy would be triple-covered. So I would always try to throw the ball to Troy and Bill would go crazy," Zolak said.

The voices of coaches were booming across the practice field.

"Get Tupa in there!" they bellowed, referring to backup quarterback Tom Tupa.

"Throw the ball where it's supposed to be thrown!" they screamed.

But Zolak kept pushing the envelope, and Troy loved it. Even on scout team, they wouldn't concede an interception. They still wanted to make a play.

"Troy always knew how to get open, no matter who was covering him in practice, whether it was Ty Law or Otis Smith," Zolak said. "He'd get in the huddle and say, 'Come on, give me this one!' And I'd continue to feed him. We would just make a ton of plays. Practice became our games; it's kind of how we got ourselves through it every day. Certain guys develop a rapport and in a weird way I had that with Troy in practice. He'd give me the wink and I knew he was going to beat that guy. I'd look the other way and throw it to Troy."

Troy believes Zolak was critical in him making the initial roster. Zolak isn't so sure.

"He was always competing, never dogged it, caught everything," Zolak said. "I don't want to say we kept each other in the league, but when you say bubble guy, you'd hear Parcells say, 'I don't know Brown, we have six receivers here, we have this fifth guy, and this guy is a veteran, so you might not make it. You better do more than catch passes!' Sure enough, Troy found ways to do other things.

"He was always a classic bubble guy. In this league, we get enamored with the statistical part of size. The receiver needed to be 6'1" or 6'2", and run a 4.6 or better. And run a good route. Troy was one of those undersized guys, but he fought through everything. He has so much heart.

"I look at him like the Tedy Bruschi of the offense in those years. I remember being at one practice in 1996 where Parcells was yelling at [defensive coordinator] Al Groh, saying, 'I don't know what you're going to do with this No. 54 [Bruschi], but you need to find a spot for him! I don't care if you stand him up or put him down.' Troy was the offensive version of that.

"He would do anything you asked him to do. I remember him always having those helmet covers on. Back in the day, when we practiced special teams, we'd have players put Velcro shells on their helmets. I never remember seeing No. 80 with Troy's helmet because he always had that shell on, or on his jersey because it was covered by a pinney. He was always on the scout team. He'd always be the opponents' top receiver from the other team, making sure the top defense would get a good look in practice."

When Zolak looks back on his nine-year career, from 1991 to 1999, playing with Troy was a highlight.

"You deal with a lot of egos in this game, but Troy was never that guy. He's one of the nicest guys on and off the field," he said. "Our conditions weren't the greatest at old Gillette Stadium. We had that old locker room underneath and that old weight room. He was one of the first guys in the weight room every day. You'd see him sweating, doing the power cleans and the squats, the same type of stuff the linemen did. We would always do these box jumps, a vertical leap type thing. Troy always stood out with that. He could just go all day. He was like Ty [Law], you'd always see them on the treadmill before and after practice."

In that 1995 preseason, Troy will never forget that long plane ride home from Oakland because when the team arrived home around 5:00 AM EST, Parcells pulled him aside and had something important to say to him: "Don't you worry about a thing. I'm going to find a spot for you on this team."

As much as it was sweet to hear, Troy almost didn't want to believe it. He didn't want to lose his edge.

Those were some of the more difficult times for any football team, when the roster is trimmed down after training camp and friends who had the same dream were sent packing. Troy knew all too well what it felt like from the year before and his costly fumble in Green Bay. You'd come into the locker room and maybe the player next to you was cleaning his things out, putting them into a large trash bag. You never knew if you'd see him again. He was that guy just the year before.

So Troy was determined to fight any feeling of comfort that he'd made it, and having Zolak in his corner helped. In one of the first practices after the final preseason game, he lit it up, with Zolak feeding him football after football, and it started turning some heads because a few of the catches were dazzling. It was one of those moments where you almost forget where you are, an out-of-body experience, and when you walk off the field you sort of realize, "I just had a great practice, this is the NFL, and maybe I not only belong but I can be a difference-maker."

That's the thing that can be a tricky balance for any player near the bottom of the roster. You need to play with confidence, but at the same time, you almost need to view yourself as not good enough because living on that edge can propel you.

Unlike his first two seasons, when he didn't register a single reception, Troy totaled 14 catches over the 1995 season. He obviously liked the idea of playing more on offense, even as his role on special teams was reduced because another "Parcells guy," running back David Meggett, had been signed to return punts and also handle some kickoffs.

Troy did have 31 kickoff returns that season, for a 21.7-yard average, but Meggett bested him with 38 for a 25.4-yard average. Meggett took all 45 punt returns that season, and was also third on the team in receptions (52) and second in rushing yards (250).

Troy also took a liking to the team's first-round draft pick that year, cornerback Ty Law, as the two have remained close friends for more than two decades.

The Patriots took a step back that season, finishing 6–10, before things exploded for the better in 1996, with the team posting an 11–5 record and advancing to Super Bowl XXXI against the Green Bay Packers in New Orleans, Louisiana.

A hotshot first-round draft pick, Terry Glenn of Ohio State, brought a new dimension to the offense that year and totaled 90 catches, as did veteran Shawn Jefferson (50 receptions) as the No. 2 receiver. By that point, Troy had pretty much graduated to the No. 3 spot on the depth chart, finding his way on the field on third down, where he and starting quarterback Drew Bledsoe would sometimes hook up for clutch plays.

For maybe the first time, Troy started to think, "This is fun!" He finished with 21 catches, which was more than the 14 he had in his first three seasons combined, as his ability to relax on the field sparked some more production. He added a career-long 51-yard kickoff return as well, which further showed his ability as a playmaker.

In practice, he was getting more repetitions and feeling like a greater part of the team. Then came maybe the only thing that he couldn't afford: an injury.

Not that Troy needed any reminders about how fragile life was in the NFL, but things were about to change again. And they weren't necessarily for the better.

Four

A NOT-SO-SUPER
EXPERIENCE

When Parcells wasn't on the team plane
after the Super Bowl, it was clear to
everyone that the end had come.

CHAPTER FOUR

A Not-So-Super Experience

Every step along the way is a progression, and if there was good news in 1996, it was that Troy wasn't too worried about getting cut by the end of the preseason. He didn't need to hear any reassuring words from Bill Parcells this time around.

The Patriots started the year 0–2 with losses at Miami and Buffalo before turning things around and making a somewhat improbable run to the Super Bowl.

Troy's final statistics—21 catches for 222 yards—were acceptable, but in truth a bit of a disappointment to him. He had hoped to do more. The one thing that made him feel a bit better about his contributions was his work on special teams; he had done some of his best work as a kickoff returner—29 returns for 634 yards and a long of 51 yards.

Of course, Troy was never one to put his personal statistics ahead of team goals. The Patriots were winning, there was good chemistry in the locker room, Parcells was making the right moves as coach, and so it created an atmosphere that was mostly happy.

Then came an unfortunate turn of events in the regular-season finale.

The Patriots were playing a road game against the Giants and Troy caught a short pass toward the sideline and was driven to the ground by a defender. Troy immediately felt something wrong; it felt like a zipper going down his crotch. He was quickly diagnosed with a groin injury and he knew it wasn't good.

When Troy got to the sideline, he immediately took one of the sleeves that players use for protection and pulled it up as far as he could. It helped slightly, but not much.

The injury overshadowed one of the more remarkable plays of his career—a 13-yard catch on third-and-13 on the game-winning drive—which he made on his back.

He finished the game, and the Patriots had a bye after that, and then it was on to the playoffs.

It was frustrating for Troy, knowing he couldn't accelerate on the field the way he wanted. Just sitting around and playing dominoes, he couldn't laugh, and it actually hurt to talk at times. Sneezing was the worst. Coughing was almost as bad. The pain was intense, irritating him constantly, and by leaning to one side it alleviated some of the sharpness of it.

But when thinking about what it would take to play in a playoff game, Troy had his doubts.

Still, when the time came, he suited up even though he clearly wasn't himself. The divisional round game against Pittsburgh was played in the fog and the Patriots won. Then the team caught a break when the fifth-seeded Jaguars upset the top-seeded Broncos in the other divisional-round game, meaning the Patriots would host Jacksonville in the AFC title game (a game they won 20–6).

Troy was devastated as the team turned its attention to the Super Bowl because nothing felt right. During an indoor practice, he caught a pass along the sideline, tapped his toes to the ground, and it was agony. He remembers it felt as if someone ripped his insides out.

Troy walked to the sideline. Bill Parcells asked where he was going.

The answer: straight to the athletic training staff so he could get treatment for the groin injury.

At that point, Troy feared the worst. He badly wanted to play in the Super Bowl, fulfilling a lifelong dream, a reminder that he had indeed arrived on the biggest of stages. At the same time, this was like trying to drive a car without a wheel. What good is that?

He was held out of practice all week, and he could sense a vibe from the coaching staff that was going to threaten his chances of playing in the game. They weren't sure how much they could depend on him and how long the groin would hold up.

Troy held out hope that the coaches would give him the green light, but by breakfast the morning of the game, he could tell where it was going to end up. That's when he saw Parcells and the coach wouldn't even look at him. From that point on, Troy figured there was no way he'd be playing in the Super Bowl.

He cried on the spot.

And as the tears flowed, he just wanted Parcells to see him, to feel the despair. "Come on, Bill! Look at me!"

Parcells, as Troy remembers it, couldn't bring himself to make eye contact over a stretch of time that might have been only five minutes or so, though it felt like an eternity. He also didn't tell Troy directly that he wouldn't play, instead leaving it to strength and conditioning coach Johnny Parker to deliver the unpleasant news.

No hard feelings, Troy said. He was just wearing his heart on his jersey sleeve and understood where Parcells was coming from: Troy was injured, couldn't practice, and there was no guarantee of how much he could be depended upon.

Everyone knows what happened next. The spot that Troy would have been playing on the kickoff coverage team was the exact area where Green Bay Packers returner Desmond Howard blazed up the field on a 99-yard kickoff return for a touchdown. That play still keeps Troy up at night sometimes, wondering if he might have been able to make a tackle on the game-turning score. Troy's injury had thrust second-year receiver Hason Graham into the spot, and the two were neighbors. Troy felt that was a tough spot to put Graham. At the same time, he had confidence that had he been in there, he would have made the tackle. He was that confident in his special-teams abilities.

To this day, he still thinks about how he would have played it— right on Howard's shoulder, a blindside type of kill shot he probably would have taken, and maybe could have even jarred the football free as well. Maybe that's the difference between winning and losing.

That feeling of guilt has never really gone away for Troy. He felt like he let the team down a bit, but if anyone could have felt the shooting pain from his groin, they would have understood.

There haven't been too many other times in Troy's life that he felt as helpless. He always felt like part of the team, but in this case, it was as if something was missing. He still pictures that play on a regular basis.

It was a crushing end of the season for Troy, and he was also crushed about the change on the sidelines—Bill Parcells out, Pete Carroll in.

Troy had sensed Parcells was going to be out, going back to his remarks about "shopping for the groceries," and for players in the building, it was easy to sense some of the tension.

Some have asked Troy how much that might have taken away from the team's preparation for the Super Bowl, the rumors circulating that Parcells was involved in a rift with owner Robert Kraft, but Troy didn't see that as a factor. It was a minor distraction, but nothing the team couldn't handle.

What was harder to digest from Troy's perspective was that the Patriots had just advanced to the Super Bowl, the team had jelled, and now they were going to start over? It seemed foolish to him.

So it was a double punch in the gut—first the Super Bowl loss when he couldn't even play, and then losing Parcells. When Parcells wasn't on the team plane after the Super Bowl, it was clear to everyone that the end had come.

That had Troy thinking about what Parcells meant to his career.

The first thing is that there are always going to be things a player doesn't like or agree with when it comes to coaching decisions, but you still respect them because they've been so great. Troy bought in to Parcells because of that, figuring he always knew what was best for him. That he gave Troy his first chance in the NFL was obviously incredibly meaningful.

Troy was never afraid of hard work, and from his view, the players who usually clashed with Parcells were those guys who didn't want to put in the time. All Troy asked for was an opportunity, a chance to give the coaches a level of comfort in putting him on the field, and Parcells provided that for him.

Like Bill Belichick later in his career, Parcells demanded players to be great. Not good. Great. You always had to do a little more. There's nothing wrong with that in Troy's mind. He was never one to take a shortcut.

With the change, Troy considered a change himself. He was a free agent and he wasn't sure if he'd be back in New England the following season.

Five

STOP PICKING ON OUR FIRST-ROUND DRAFT CHOICE!

At times Troy would want to scream out,
"Do something! Send someone home!
Make a statement!"

CHAPTER FIVE

Stop Picking on Our First-Round Draft Choice!

Between the Patriots' head-coaching change and his groin injury, Troy viewed his future as uncertain. He didn't think the injury was career-threatening and he also didn't know how long he'd be in New England.

There were a few times over his Patriots career when he seriously considered playing elsewhere and this was one of them. He took a visit to the Carolina Panthers that off-season, and given how close they were to his roots, there was real interest in possibly signing with them. The Kansas City Chiefs were another team in the mix.

Later in his career, Troy considered what it would be like to play elsewhere but didn't follow through on it because he had developed such strong ties to New England. This was different. He was just four years in and, had things worked out differently, he easily could have seen himself playing for the Panthers, who were located a little less than two hours from his hometown. Plus, they were a good, young team that had advanced to the NFC Championship Game the year before. Troy liked their direction, and he wasn't sure about the direction of the Patriots.

If not for the Patriots making an aggressive push to retain him, Troy probably would have been gone and his Patriots Hall of Fame story never would have come to fruition.

That was his first notable contract and it helped him buy his mother, Richadean, her first home.

Before doing so, he called Chris Scelfo, the coach who had recruited him to Marshall, looking for a little guidance. Troy wasn't sure of all the specifics, such as the mortgage process, and figured Scelfo might be able to help.

In a sense, the conversation reflected the special bond that sometimes exists between a player and coach. Almost six or seven years after they first met, they were still close, the coach serving as a father figure of sorts.

To Scelfo, the conversation also highlighted one of the lighthearted things he often ribs Troy about—how he's a notorious saver of money. One joke is that Troy has fishhooks in his pockets when it comes to money.

The cost of the home was $30,000.

When Scelfo learned what Troy had saved in the bank, and that he could pay for the home without a mortgage, he helped Troy follow through with the gesture that meant so much to Richadean and her son.

That was one of the highlights for Troy in those years. Still, that time football-wise from 1997 to 1999 under Pete Carroll wasn't easy for Troy.

It wasn't that he didn't like Carroll. It was just that Carroll seemed to be put in a tough situation, taking over a team that had just been to the Super Bowl, and there were a lot of changes being made. It didn't make sense to Troy, almost as if there was a feeling this was a 7–9 team instead of a Super Bowl contender. It was also clear that Carroll didn't have a lot of clout with those decisions.

Unlike Parcells, Troy never really hit it off with Carroll. He felt that Carroll catered too much to superstar players, and he wasn't one of them.

For example, Troy remembers when Carroll would run a team meeting and talk about how disappointed he was when a player was late to a meeting. He'd call some players out, but seldom, if ever, one of the superstars, according to Troy. To himself, Troy would say, "Hey, what about one of your players who just strolled in late? He messed up. Why aren't you saying something about him?" Troy had hoped to see more action from Carroll, maybe making an example of one of the players he viewed as a "Carroll guy," but it didn't happen.

Troy just never felt things meshed with him and Carroll and most of his staff. He appreciated being brought back on a fair free-agent contract, but the sense he wasn't one of Carroll's guys was hard to overcome. Part of that was that the club kept bringing in wide receivers. He just felt he could never win over the coaching staff.

In 1997, Troy looked at the roster and the salaries of each receiver, thinking something had to give. Terry Glenn, the team's first-round draft pick from the year before, was entrenched. He was making good money. So were Vincent Brisby and Shawn Jefferson. So that's three receivers earning more than $1 million.

At that point, he was actually second-guessing his decision to return, wondering if he should have followed through with the opportunity in Carolina.

Then he reminded himself of what had gotten him to that point and decided the better approach would be to make the best of the situation. Learning a new offense, he produced 41 receptions for 607 yards that season, which were the best numbers of his career. He wasn't a starter, but then-offensive coordinator Larry Kennan seemed to take a liking to him.

That seemed to be different from the relationship that Kennan had with Terry Glenn, who was a difficult personality to manage in Troy's view. One example was how Glenn would be on his phone in the receivers' meeting while everybody else was watching film. Glenn would also lay on the floor in the old meeting rooms at Foxboro Stadium.

Every once in a while, receivers coach Steve Walters attempted to engage Glenn, but it didn't lead to anything productive. The team ended up moving Ivan Fears to coach receivers, but that didn't make a big difference.

Glenn could have had a great career in Troy's eyes, had he worked at things a bit more. Troy saw a lot of wasted potential there.

So back to Carroll, it was those type of things that pretty much doomed him from the beginning. He struggled to handle players like Terry Glenn, and that trickled down to the position coaches. When Glenn pulled stuff like that, nothing ever seemed to happen to him until a long overdue suspension. But by that point, it was too late.

Everyone was frustrated over Glenn.

In times like that, Troy buckled down and took the approach that he could only control his own situation. He worked hard to try not to get caught up in the locker-room chatter about who was getting the ball and who wasn't, focusing instead on any additional repetitions he could get on the practice field. When he sensed that some of his teammates might be taking their foot off the gas pedal at practice, he tried to push his down harder on the accelerator.

That created a little bit of a divide between him and some others in the locker room. Troy himself felt like a misfit of sorts, and he took a ribbing from some teammates.

The whole vibe around the team was so different from what he had experienced the year before. The difference between Carroll and Parcells was extreme, and that carried over into the locker room as well. Troy still couldn't figure out why there were so many personnel changes that year, given that the 1996 team had been so successful.

The team got younger, filled with draft picks, many of whom didn't meet expectations. Some of those youngsters, from Troy's view, didn't seem to respect Carroll enough, and the job itself.

Maybe, Troy thought, it was a case of Carroll's background and coming from a San Francisco 49ers team that had established players like John Taylor, Jerry Rice, and Joe Montana, who could police themselves and knew how to work and prepare. As defensive coordinator with those teams, maybe he didn't have to stay on top of them all the time.

Contrast that to two of the top draft picks in Carroll's first year—cornerback Chris Canty of Kansas State and safety Chris Carter of Texas—and it was clear they needed someone who wasn't afraid to drop the hammer on them. Troy viewed them as players who did what they wanted and weren't ready for games.

In fact, Scott Zolak, the backup quarterback who developed a rapport with Troy in practice that Troy believes was critical in him sticking on the roster initially, recalls the two being called in for a chat with Pete Carroll.

"This is my favorite Troy story," Zolak recalled. "We had drafted Chris Canty No. 1 and Troy and I had a lot of success against him in practice. So at one point, Pete Carroll sat us down and said, 'Guys, could you please stop throwing at our first-round pick because you're really making him look bad!'"

Troy and Zolak didn't think Carroll was kidding, either.

In Troy's view, that was a big difference between the Parcells years and the Carroll years. One coach was pushing everyone to their limits. The other coach, not so much.

So it was no surprise to Troy that the Patriots took a step back that year, even though they made the playoffs. The overall discipline wasn't there and everything seemed like such a struggle.

For Troy, this was nothing personal with Carroll. He liked him and believed that if the team had been more mature, keeping some more of the players from the 1996 squad, there was a chance for better results. Having more seasoned professionals can help a team through some tough times, and also influence some of the more immature players.

Looking back on Carroll's three years, Troy saw things heading in the wrong direction—two playoff games, one playoff game, then missing the playoffs altogether. He noticed a general decline in personnel and also felt like Carroll could have been tougher on players.

That was a first-hand experience for Troy of how a culture can erode and it can be okay for players to pretty much stop caring. He was shocked to see players arriving late for meetings, the locker room turning from neat and orderly to a mess, and teammates bringing shopping bags on road trips.

At times Troy would want to scream out, "Do something! Send someone home! Make a statement!"

But he didn't feel it was his place to express those feelings, even though he knew there were others around him who agreed. Then he saw others who didn't mind it because they didn't have to be accountable. To some, it was show up, get paid, go home. Troy didn't see the game respected at the level it should have been.

He couldn't bring himself to think along those lines, and he missed some of his old teammates from the '96 squad, some of the same guys who used to hang around, play dominoes and Scrabble. That type of camaraderie was harder to find in those days. The attitude of the building had changed and Troy didn't feel the same type of confidence going into games.

He had heard the stories about players going behind Carroll's back and up to the office of vice president of player personnel Bobby Grier, and he knew it happened with one player in particular—Terry Glenn. If Glenn didn't like the game plan, he could be seen crumpling it up and throwing it into the trash can. Troy watched Glenn lying on the floor, uninterested while others were watching film and learning the game plan. Stories of him going up to Grier's office were shared among players.

When it seemed that the coaching staff was calling plays specifically to appease Glenn, it bothered Troy as much as anything else. It was basically rewarding the behavior. He knew how something like that would be handled under Parcells.

Troy took note of how Glenn had all the talent anyone could ask for, but fell short in most other areas. Those were the areas that Troy prided himself in, which made it all the more frustrating for him.

In 1998, new offensive coordinator Ernie Zampese had more of a take-charge approach, and he seemed to like Troy. That was welcomed by Troy, but at the same time, another significant financial investment was made in free-agent receiver Brian Stablein.

Troy couldn't help but ask, "What do I need to do here?"

Zampese, who Troy felt was the one coach who believed in him, told him to just be himself, and with Drew Bledsoe having a growing confidence in him, he still made somewhat of a mark—23 catches in 1998 and 36 in 1999.

When Troy looked at his career at that point, he had been through the survival stage just to earn a roster spot as a rookie. Then came the big dip in Year 2 when he thought his NFL dream was over, only to have it revived midseason. There was the big disappointment of not being able to play in the Super Bowl, and then the struggle of the Pete Carroll years.

Where it would all lead from there, he wasn't sure. But he was thrilled to learn that the team's next coach was Bill Belichick, which gave him hope that better days were ahead.

Six

A CAREER
BREAKTHROUGH
IN YEAR 8

"I'm tired of losing!" he said to his teammates
as tears started to stream down his face.

CHAPTER SIX

A Career Breakthrough in Year 8

It didn't take long for Troy to realize things were going to be different with the Patriots in 2000. He felt the off-season practices were much more organized and crisp, and more serious than they were under the Pete Carroll regime. He also felt his input was more valued by the coaching staff.

As a free agent that off-season, Troy was visiting with the Kansas City Chiefs when he received a phone call from Bill Belichick and his offensive coordinator, Charlie Weis. They told him they wanted him back and promised him that he'd have an opportunity to be a starter.

"We think you have what it takes to be one of our guys," they told him, reflecting some internal conversations in which Belichick and Weis viewed Troy as a solid player who had yet to receive a full-fledged opportunity to show what he could do as a slot receiver and deceptive big-play receiver. Belichick, in particular, remembered how hard it was for defensive backs to cover Troy in practice in 1996, the year Belichick was an assistant coach on Parcells' staff.

Those words were music to Troy's ears because he never felt that vibe from Carroll or vice president of player personnel Bobby Grier.

In fact, he remembers almost wanting to come to blows with Carroll when Troy was called for holding and Carroll was riding him on the sidelines in front of his teammates. Besides the fact that the holding call seemed borderline to him, to Troy, it was one of the only times Carroll had ever really addressed him like that.

The methods seemed inconsistent to him—Carroll didn't get on every player like that—and Troy stewed when it happened.

With Belichick and Weis, they might rip into you, but you knew they were doing it to everyone. Sort of like the Parcells years when he rankled Drew Bledsoe often.

Troy hadn't interacted much with Belichick in 1996, the one year Belichick served as a defensive assistant on Parcells' Patriots staff. In fact, Troy doesn't remember many players speaking with him, as he was a coach who seemed to blend into the background more than anything else. But as he later found out, Belichick was always watching everything and was a copious note-taker.

It turns out the Patriots' free-agent offer was better than the Chiefs' offer, so Troy decided to stick with the Patriots, and he was happy that's the way it unfolded because he had somewhat of a connection with Weis (who was on Parcells' staff in New England) and some other assistants.

Troy knew the coaching staff was true to its word when it cut former second-round draft choice Vincent Brisby. That's one of the things Belichick has always stressed; it doesn't matter how you arrived in terms of draft status, your place on the roster will be determined by how you perform.

Weis' offensive system had some carryover from Ernie Zampese's system under Pete Carroll, so Troy felt comfortable in that area as well. He was making plays, getting plenty of opportunites, and feeling good about his standing. In fact, Weis would sometimes ask him the plays he liked to run. What Troy liked were the option plays over the middle, which gave him a chance to read the defense and get open. They are the same routes that Wes Welker would later run with great success during his Patriots career (2007–2012).

That's when Troy knew things were different—both from a Patriots perspective and for himself. The coaching was better and he felt more valued. Weis, he felt, made him a better player as he had a sharp mind for offensive football, not to mention a sharp tongue. He could really lay into players, although he seemed to soften a bit in that area in his second coaching stint with the Patriots.

There was another subplot to that 2000 season. It was with a rookie quarterback named Tom Brady.

The 199th draft pick out of Michigan hardly looked like a football player when Troy first laid eyes on him that year. He was skinny, lanky, and didn't inspire much confidence from the casual eye test.

Yet when he took the field, Brady carried himself with the confidence of an All-Pro, even that first year. One time, Troy remembers talking with fellow receiver Vincent Brisby about how Brady was following him down the field and telling him how precisely he wanted routes run. Brisby's first thought was, "Who does this guy think he is?"

But the more they practiced with him, the more they came to respect the approach. It wasn't as if Brady was disrespecting the receivers as players, but he was demanding in a way that made you take notice. Usually players at that stage of their careers keep quiet, take their reps, and fall into line. But not Brady.

As America later discovered, that was just who Brady was, whether he was the fourth-stringer, second-stringer, or surprise Super Bowl winner in 2001. He might have driven a hard bargain on the field, but he backed it up because he held himself to the same high standard. He would tell receivers what he wanted, but at the same time he'd tell them, "This is what you should expect out of me." Players like Troy also took note that Brady was a weight-room junkie, outworking pretty much everyone. That was part of what made him such a great leader.

Still, Troy wondered that first year if such a skinny prospect could ultimately withstand the physical toll of the NFL.

For Troy himself, he felt momentum building in 2000, starting with the financial security of his free-agent contract, which helped him relax a bit on the field. He liked the feeling that he had a bit of a personal stake in the fortunes of the team and his statistics were career-bests.

He had a team-high 83 receptions for 944 yards and four touchdowns that year, to go along with 39 punt returns for 504 yards and one touchdown.

For perspective, Troy had totaled 127 receptions in his first seven NFL seasons combined. So this was a major breakthrough.

The Patriots finished 5–11 that season, but there was a feeling that the team was on the right track. In fact, it was notable to Troy how an 8–8 season under Pete Carroll in 1999 might have looked better on paper, but it felt much worse than the five-win 2000 campaign while going through it.

Troy's feeling as a stakeholder in the team's success was evidenced when he did something he'd seldom do over his career: stand in front of the team and make a speech. That wasn't his thing, but something overcame him that year and he let it rip before a home game.

"I'm tired of losing!" he said to his teammates as tears started to stream down his face. "We've got to do something about this!"

It's a speech that teammates would later rib Troy about, but it also showed how much he cared. Later, Belichick pulled him aside and praised him for the words.

Sure, he had more money in his bank account than ever before. And it also felt great to be producing on the field. But he was driven by more than that, and it's no wonder he would later become one of Belichick's favorite players to coach.

The Patriots finished that year with three wins in their final six games. Things were on the rise. It was a near perfect year for Troy, except for one major misstep.

* * *

No one is perfect, and if there is a lesson that Troy tries to teach his own children, it's to be accountable when you fall into that category.

Maybe the biggest mistake of Troy's career came during that 2000 season.

It was mid-December and the Patriots were playing a road game in western New York against the Buffalo Bills. If you've ever been to Orchard Park, New York, at that time of year, well, you know it's not exactly the best conditions. On this day, it was cold, windy, and icy, and the way Troy remembers it, Bill Belichick gave players the option to drive if they weren't comfortable flying home.

Troy never liked flying, so it was a no-brainer for him to step off the plane when an announcement was made that if winds were deemed to be unsafe, the plane wouldn't take off. With winds already in the 30 mile-per-hour range, Troy decided to play it safe. So did teammates Ty Law and Terry Glenn.

Troy figured more players would have done the same, but it turned out they were the only ones. And soon enough, they were in the headlines for the wrong reasons.

The three had taken a bus and were in downtown Buffalo, when they decided to cross the border into Canada. They ended up at a gentleman's lounge, and one thing led to another, and Troy remembers Ty Law getting separated from him and Terry Glenn.

This put Troy in a tough spot. He tried to contact Ty—they had cell phones at the time—but couldn't make the connection. So at that point, it was just him and Terry Glenn and Terry urged him to leave. Troy didn't want to do so, as he was worried about Ty's whereabouts, but that's what they did. They decided to head to the airport to fly home, which is when they bumped into several reporters who had covered the Patriots-Bills game the day before. The reporters were flying home themselves.

Imagine that type of thing happening in today's media culture with Twitter and social media. It would have blown up. And this one blew up too, but just 2000-style, with big newspaper headlines and newscasts leading with reports of Ty Law across the border getting mixed up in some bad stuff.

When Troy saw that on television, he knew he was going to be in hot water with Belichick. So he called Terry Glenn and told him that the two of them had to go see Belichick and explain what happened.

That was one of the toughest things he ever had to do, explaining that they didn't want to leave their teammate behind, but got caught in a bad spot, and ultimately were accountable for their actions.

Belichick, rightfully so, was furious. His message to them was that they were pulling the team down.

Troy was devastated and also felt stories in the local newspapers were misrepresenting his role in what had unfolded, connecting him to drugs. Still, he knew he never should have put himself in that situation and he held himself accountable.

In those types of situations, you have to take control and he didn't. He was torn between finding his friend in an unfamiliar place and getting back to town on time.

The whole thing was just an unfortunate turn of events from start to finish. If he had just stayed on the plane in the first place, none of it would have happened.

He messed up. He knew it.

Now he had to win back some of the trust he had developed with Belichick.

Seven

AN UNFORGETTABLE
2001 SEASON

Troy had been on the field for the play, so he ran over to check on Bledsoe. Drew's eyes were glossed over, the facemask looked bent, and he was sort of rocking himself back and forth.

CHAPTER SEVEN

An Unforgettable 2001 Season

The 2000 season had ended with a 27–24 loss to the Miami Dolphins at Foxboro Stadium. It was a strange game in the sense that officials had players return to the field after leaving for the locker room, because there was still time on the clock. Some players didn't even have their uniforms on when they came back out.

But what Troy remembered even more about that game was the loud cheering from the visitors' locker room, which could easily be heard through the thin walls at the Patriots' home stadium. With the victory, the Dolphins had clinched the AFC East championship and they were naturally excited.

That's when safety Lawyer Milloy stood up and said to his teammates, "Listen to that noise. Remember it. Let's never feel this way again. That should be us!"

The Patriots, to the surprise of America, would be that team in 2001.

Troy was closing on his 30th birthday, his career clock was ticking, and he only wished he had a chance to play under Belichick, Weis, and the coaching staff earlier and more consistently.

The '01 season got off to a heartbreaking start when quarterbacks coach Dick Rehbein passed away. Troy remembers how respected Rehbein was. That season was, in part, dedicated to his memory. A 23–17 season-opening loss to Cincinnati got things off on the wrong foot and then Week 2 games were canceled due to the terrorist attacks of September 11.

The attacks occurred on Tuesday, the players' day off, and when everyone arrived for work the following day, Troy remembers everyone rallying around offensive lineman Joe Andruzzi, whose brothers were New York City firefighters. There was naturally concern about their safety.

Players were soon told that everything was being shut down and that players should return home to their loved ones. So Troy loaded up his car and drove 13 hours straight to West Virginia. That's where he wanted to be, and the ride was unforgettable, especially passing through New York.

Upon returning to Foxborough, Troy found it hard to get restarted and it showed on the field in the team's next game, against the New York Jets at home. The game, of course, was remembered for the crunching hit that linebacker Mo Lewis delivered on quarterback Drew Bledsoe. Troy was about 15 to 20 yards away from the hit, but the sound of it was crystal clear. Thud! Bang!

It almost sounded like a gun had been fired off.

Troy had been on the field for the play, so he ran over to check on Bledsoe. Drew's eyes were glossed over, the facemask looked bent, and he was sort of rocking himself back and forth. As a player, those are the moments that are always tough and there is no hesitation in calling for the doctors. Troy knew it wasn't good. It was scary.

But Troy didn't think Bledsoe's life was in any sort of danger, as players would later discover was the case. Bledsoe actually tried to play through the injury at one point, but Troy could tell when he was in the huddle that he wasn't right. So the decision was made to go with Tom Brady, the confident kid who had made an impression on Troy and others early in his rookie 2000 season.

Everyone knows what unfolded from there, but at the time, Troy's real concern was with his friend Bledsoe, who was taken to the hospital and the words "internal bleeding" were being discussed among teammates.

Bledsoe would ultimately recover, but would the Patriots? That was the question at the time, as the team wasn't playing particularly well and hadn't carried over its momentum from the end of the 2000 season. And now they were turning to an untested quarterback who hadn't started an NFL game.

Players hid any doubts they might have had and did their best to rally behind Brady. That was the message from Belichick, who simply said, "Tom is our quarterback now. We're going to play with who we have." That is pretty much Belichick's message with every injury situation, but this one was obviously bigger than most.

There was no fire-and-brimstone speech or anything like that, as Troy recalls it; just business as usual, trying to keep things as normal as possible. Troy thought about what might have unfolded if the same thing happened a few years earlier under Pete Carroll. His conclusion was that it would have been a disaster because they didn't have the needed veteran leadership to pull through.

But this 2001 team was different, as Belichick and vice president of player personnel Scott Pioli had brought in respected players like Roman Phifer, Bobby Hamilton, Mike Vrabel, and Anthony Pleasant. Troy remembers them having a calming type effect on the locker room. They helped change the culture, and replaced younger players like Andy Katzenmoyer, who were now out of the program. Those players became a sounding board for many, specifically when it came to what it was like playing for Belichick and in such a demanding environment. They were the types of players Troy felt were missing from the Pete Carroll era (1997–1999).

Up to that point, Troy had found some motivation in competing against his teammate Terry Glenn, who was basically the opposite of him in terms of how he came into the NFL. Glenn was a first-round pick, which means he had a significantly larger margin for error than Troy did over his career. Glenn, to be fair, was also more naturally gifted from an athletic standpoint than Troy.

But when it came to work ethic and quiet leadership, it wasn't a contest. Troy was the choice every time.

Still, he'd hear comments like, "We don't win that game without Terry," and it would fuel him. Soon enough, Glenn's actions caught up to him; he was suspended by Bill Belichick and the organization for the 2001 season. Glenn was initially suspended for the first four games of that year by the NFL for violating the substance abuse policy, and the team basically decided it didn't want him back at all.

The club had previously signed Glenn to a six-year, $50 million contract and withheld the remaining portion of his signing bonus. Players seemed relieved at the suspension, with fiery safety Lawyer

Milloy saying, "It's just a cancer to us right now. As a whole, that situation probably needed to die as soon as possible."

That's when Troy knew the Patriots team had a chance to win, because that was the type of leadership he felt was missing from the prior regime. Thus, he was optimistic, even though the team's current outlook wasn't exactly promising.

It was Week 3 of the 2001 season, the Patriots were 0–2, and they had a change at the game's most important position—Tom Brady in for Drew Bledsoe at quarterback. Not exactly a rosy picture as they prepared for a home game against Peyton Manning and the Indianapolis Colts. Manning, of course, had been the No. 1 overall pick of the 1998 draft.

Oh, by the way, the Colts had won their first two games that season over the Jets (45–24) and Bills (42–26).

What Troy remembers most about that week with the Patriots was veteran linebacker Bryan Cox assuming a more vocal role from a leadership perspective. If Troy was the silent type, Cox was a talker. Boy, he could come up with some stuff when speaking with teammates. Every team has players like that, but here's the key: If you're going to talk, you better be prepared to back it up.

Cox did that, delivering a hit on Colts receiver Jerome Pathon over the middle in that game against the Colts that not only rocked Pathon, but sent a message to the rest of his teammates. Troy loved it. The hit basically was interpreted this way: "We might be 0–2, we might have lost our quarterback, but we're going to fight like heck because we're still a tough football team!"

To Troy, the hit gave players confidence that they could overcome the adverse situation they put themselves in—and that injuries had contributed to creating—early that season. They crunched the Colts 44–13 to get their season back on track.

Then three weeks later, when the Patriots recorded a 38–17 road win over that same Colts team, Troy was on the receiving end of a 60-yard touchdown pass from receiver David Patten. That was a razzle-dazzle play in which quarterback Tom Brady lateraled to Patten, who then found a streaking Brown down the field.

With a record of 5–4, the Patriots had a telling home matchup with the St. Louis Rams on November 18. The defending Super Bowl champion Rams were nicknamed "The Greatest Show on Turf" because of their prolific passing offense and they were hard to stop, as evidenced by their 7–1 record. They were averaging a whopping 31.8 points per game at that point and the hype around them—with quarterback Kurt Warner, running back Marshall Faulk, and receiver Isaac Bruce, among others—was well deserved.

Playing on Foxboro Stadium's natural grass surface, "the Greatest Show on Turf" produced 24 points in a hard-fought 24–17 victory. There are no moral victories in football, but to Troy and the Patriots, that was as close as it came. Troy said to himself, "If that's the best team in football, and we can hang that close to them, maybe we have something special here too."

The Patriots went on to win their final six regular-season games to finish 11–5, and several were close calls, such as a 27–16 win at home over the Cleveland Browns on December 9. Troy delivered the game-turning play, an 85-yard punt return for a touchdown to break open a 10–10 game late in the second quarter. Sensational blocking, he recalled. The play was critical because neither team had been able to sustain much offense, and Troy's burst up the middle of the field provided a boost on a day in which the offense wasn't playing particularly well (the Browns had returned an interception for a touchdown).

The Patriots also needed some good fortune in that stretch, and they got it in a 12–9 win over the Bills the following week—Troy's first return to western New York since his regrettable trip there in 2000. In the game, fellow receiver David Patten had caught a ball along the sideline and gotten knocked out cold by defensive back Keion Carpenter before fumbling. Patten landed with a thud, the ball resting underneath his legs as the upper part of his body touched the out-of-bounds marker.

The Bills tried to pick up the football and run with it, but since Patten was technically out of bounds and making contact with the football under his legs, the play was over.

The score was tied at 9 at the time, but with their good fortune, the Patriots extended the drive and kicked what turned out to be the game-winning field goal.

That season ended differently than most, with a bye week in late December and then the regular-season finale January 6 in Carolina. That game against Carolina was supposed to be played in the second week of the season but was postponed because of the September 11 attacks.

The Patriots ripped off six straight wins to finish the season, and if one thing stood out to Troy it was how the focus on situational football was paying off. That is a Bill Belichick staple, the mastery of all the different situations that can come up at any point in a game. Practices would be filled with those types of situations, Belichick calling them out, and players would be forced to react. It's the combination of physical and mental execution.

That was sort of what that Patriots team hung its hat on because it wasn't like they were "the Greatest Show on Turf" or anything like that. But converting in the key situations, such as third downs and short yardage; relying on an Antowain Smith–led running attack; and playing good complementary football with the offense, defense, and special teams, helped pull them through in tight games.

And, of course, a little good fortune helped too, as everyone would soon see in the playoffs.

* * *

Troy and the Patriots entered their divisional-round playoff game against the Oakland Raiders with confidence. The Raiders had the long trip to town after playing the weekend before at home (a 38–24 win over the Jets) and the weather called for snow. The Patriots were used to playing in the snow; the Raiders not so much.

But that confidence quickly evaporated as the Raiders effectively used the short passing game to keep the Patriots off balance. It was a lot of catch-and-run stuff. Veteran receivers Jerry Rice and Tim Brown were rising up in the moment and the Patriots were in trouble, down 13–3 in the third quarter.

It wasn't a laughing matter, but Troy did get a chuckle when Tom Brady face-planted after his six-yard touchdown run midway through the fourth quarter when he attempted to spike the ball.

That touchdown brought the Patriots within three points and ultimately set up the play everyone remembers—the tuck rule call. Troy saw it all unfold in slow motion—Brady dropping back to pass, patting the ball, and Raiders defensive back Charles Woodson screaming off the edge. Troy wanted to scream in Brady's direction, but that wouldn't have made a difference.

Bam! Woodson delivered the hit, the ball was jarred free and the Raiders recovered to essentially seal the upset victory. To Troy, it sure looked like a fumble. He didn't know about the "Tuck Rule," so he walked off the field, his head down, shoulders slumped, thinking this was it. The seven-game winning streak was coming to an end.

Troy did what most players do in moments like those; he tried to come to grips with his frustrations. The Patriots had won seven games in a row, had a great opportunity, and they let it slip through their grasp. Terrible, he thought. When you have so many things working in your favor—home game, snow, momentum—and you just let that opportunity get away from you, it truly stings.

Then Troy thought to himself, "Why is referee Walt Coleman going to instant replay on this fumble?" A fumble is a fumble, he figured.

That's when a few teammates came over to tell him that there was a chance Brady's arm was going forward and maybe it wasn't a fumble. Troy remembers a general feeling of confusion among players. He didn't want to get his hopes us, convinced that there was no chance this was going to go the Patriots' way.

Then he suddenly realized that he and the Patriots had their "Bingo!" moment, with Coleman ruling that Brady's arm wasn't going forward, yet since he was in the act of bringing the ball back to his body after the pump fake, it was a tuck.

The first time Troy had heard of the "Tuck Rule" was at that moment. People say you don't appreciate what you have until it's gone, and that perfectly describes Troy's emotions at that time. He thought the season was over, but now having a chance to keep it alive, he felt revived.

Meanwhile, Troy noticed the Raiders seemed to be coming unraveled, still bickering about the call, their focus tested because just as the Patriots thought their season was over, Oakland players had thought they were advancing to the AFC Championship Game.

Even though the Patriots trailed at that point, 13–10, Troy felt momentum on their side. Watching tight end Jermaine Wiggins and fellow receiver David Patten make big catch after big catch had him appreciating being in the moment.

The climax came when kicker Adam Vinatieri delivered one of the greatest field goals in the history of the NFL, if not the greatest— a 45-yarder through the snow to tie the game at 13. Often overlooked is that Troy had a 27-yard punt return to help put the Patriots in that position (he fumbled at the end, with Larry Izzo recovering). As Vinatieri lined up the kick, Troy sat down beside his good friend Ty Law on the Patriots' bench and the two prayed together.

"[Vinatieri]'s from South Dakota. He's used to this weather," one of them quipped.

Troy can still replay the kick in his head as if it happened yesterday—it was low, the snow was coming down, the wind tricky. He was a bit puzzled as to why the Raiders didn't make more of an effort to block it more aggressively, to get their hands up into the flight path. But that still required a terrific kick and Vinatieri delivered. Troy marveled at his decision to go with the low trajectory, almost like a golf shot driven into the wind.

Troy used the word "destiny" at that point to describe what was happening to the Patriots. The seven wins to finish the regular season. The tuck rule (which was later eliminated by the NFL). And now this. Long snapper Lonie Paxton was making snow angels on the field as part of the celebration of what Troy calls one of the most memorable games in which he's played.

Years later, Patriots owner Robert Kraft received a framed picture from then-Raiders coach Jon Gruden that now hangs in his spacious office. The picture is of Tom Brady being hit by Charles Woodson, the ball dislodged from his grasp on the play that referee Walt Coleman determined the tuck rule would keep the ball in the Patriots' possession. Gruden signed the photo with this message: "It was a fumble."

To advance to the Super Bowl, it would require a victory at Pittsburgh against the Steelers and this is what Troy remembers about the vibe around the team: There was a large chip on their collective shoulder.

Bill Belichick stoked those emotions by pointing out what players were saying in Pittsburgh. Patriots players were told about how Steelers players had been given a day off to pack for the Super Bowl and make arrangements, and Troy even remembers hearing some of that when he turned on ESPN. Some even went so far as to tell players that the Steelers already had their AFC championship T-shirts printed up, which was stretching the truth slightly because all those shirts, for all teams, are made in advance. But players didn't know it at the time and it fueled them that much more.

Belichick played it up big behind the scenes. Troy sensed that he took it personal, too.

When Troy woke up the morning of the game, the weather couldn't have been any better. One week after a snowy divisional round game against the Raiders, it was 50 degrees and sunny. It was almost as if the forecast was a gift to the referee that day, Ed Hochuli, who is known for his large biceps and tight sleeveless shirts.

Troy obviously didn't know it at the time, but he was about to deliver some of the most memorable plays of his career. He remembers not only the excitement of the moment, but the tension of it as well. If the Patriots were motivated by all the Steelers' chatter about the Super Bowl, it turned to semi-rage in pre-game warmups when Pittsburgh running back Amos Zereoue deliberately kicked the ball off Adam Vinatieri's tee.

Meanwhile, outspoken Steelers outside linebacker Joey Porter gazed to the Patriots' side of the field in warmups, pointing his finger, and telling anyone who would listen how he planned to pummel them when the game started.

In situations like that, it helps to have a player like Bryan Cox on your team. Cox, who sparked the entire 2001 season with the big hit against Colts receiver Jerome Pathon in Week 3, answered Porter word for word. The two kept yelling at each other, all the way up to the coin toss.

If Cox helped set the tone that the Patriots weren't going to back down, Troy carried that over on the field by returning a punt 55 yards for a touchdown at the 3:42 mark of the first quarter. All week, he had studied Pittsburgh punter Josh Miller (who would later become a teammate in New England) and how he was effective at manipulating the direction of the ball, so opportunities might be limited for big returns.

The touchdown return almost didn't happen, as Miller had previously delivered a 64-yard punt that got past Troy and would have spotted the ball deeper in Patriots territory. Yet an illegal procedure penalty on Steelers coverage player Troy Edwards for going out of bounds and returning to the field of play led to a re-kick.

Steelers coach Bill Cowher was later adamant that officials spotted the ball on the wrong hashmark for the re-kick, which might have contributed to Miller's second punt coming right down the middle of the field, making a return possible for Troy.

Cowher fumed afterward, saying, "In my mind, that's inexcusable."

Meanwhile, Troy surged up the middle and no one was catching him. The Patriots led 7–0, giving them an early cushion that provided some form of comfort when the unexpected unfolded.

When quarterback Tom Brady injured his ankle, veteran Drew Bledsoe took over. Brady vs. Bledsoe had been a hot-button storyline in New England that year. When Brady took over for Bledsoe in Week 3, the question had lingered on what would happen when Bledsoe returned to full health. That divided some in the media, creating a Bledsoe camp (players shouldn't lose their job due to injury) and a Brady camp (ride the hot hand).

Troy obviously had a strong connection with Bledsoe from having joined the Patriots at the same time in 1993. He also loved the confidence and command that Brady brought to the huddle, which everyone could see early in his rookie season of 2000.

For Troy, there was something special about what unfolded that day because Bledsoe—who handled himself with class in a tough situation—was summoned off the bench to help rescue the team. Troy could never forget the image of Bledsoe jogging onto the field with a certain swagger, looking in the eyes of his teammates in the huddle and confidently saying, "Let's win this!"

When Bledsoe delivered an 11-yard touchdown pass to receiver David Patten in the back of the end zone with 58 seconds remaining in the second quarter, it gave the Patriots a 14–3 lead.

As if this Hollywood script needed any more twists, Bledsoe also absorbed a bone-rattling hit from Steelers cornerback Chad Brown after being forced to run, which had everyone thinking back to how Bledsoe was hurt on a similar play earlier in the year. For a split second, everyone held their breath, wondering if this was going to be a carbon copy of the scary Mo Lewis hit. But Bledsoe popped back up and that galvanized the team further.

Troy was a major part of what turned out to be a 24–17 victory, first with the punt return for a touchdown and then when the Steelers attempted a 34-yard field goal in the third quarter that was blocked. Troy was first to pick up the football, doing so in stride, and after running for about 10 yards he smartly lateraled it behind him to Antwan Harris, who raced 49 yards for a touchdown. That gave the Patriots a 21–3 lead.

Later, Harris would explain, "I saw Troy pick up the ball and I yelled his name about six times. He pitched me the ball and it was history from there."

Bill Belichick often preaches the importance of all three phases of the game—offense, defense, and special teams—and this was one of those games that reinforced the message. To score 14 points on special teams to advance to the Super Bowl was sweet, especially the way the Steelers had seemed so confident leading into the game.

Pittsburgh was stunned, and the Cinderella ride to the Super Bowl continued. It was all coming full circle now, a rematch against the St. Louis Rams and "the Greatest Show on Turf."

Troy couldn't wait for the chance to play on such a big stage, especially considering the last time he had a chance—in 1996—he missed the game because of injury.

* * *

Unlike most years, when there are two weeks between the conference championship games and Super Bowl, the Patriots and Rams only had one week. That made it a blur of a week for Troy and his teammates.

They quickly arrived in New Orleans for the traditional media build-up to the game, and Bill Belichick was decisive in naming Tom Brady his starting quarterback. Troy felt that was important for players to hear, too, so there was no drama. Drew Bledsoe had done an admirable job coming off the bench in the AFC title game when Brady hurt his ankle, and there would have been confidence if he was needed again. But Brady had proven he was deserving of the job.

Troy was one of five captains on the team that year and one of the things he'll never forget was the weekly captains' meeting with Bill Belichick a few days before the Super Bowl. Belichick, as Troy remembers it, asked the captains how they should handle pre-game introductions. Because only the offense or defense could be introduced, one side would get the short straw.

Troy doesn't remember who it was—maybe linebacker Bryan Cox—but someone suggested that the team continue to do what it had all season by being introduced as a team. "Why change now?" they said.

Belichick liked it, the NFL didn't, but the decision summed up part of what made that 2001 team so special. It wasn't the most talented group of players. But it was a true team.

The Patriots were heavy underdogs but Troy remembers a confidence among players, even though a dome game on artificial turf against "the Greatest Show on Turf" wasn't necessarily a great matchup. What seemed to add to the Patriots' confidence was the fact they had played the Rams so tough in mid-November. The Patriots had familiarity with a lot of their personnel.

Whereas the week before, Bill Belichick had riled up players by telling them about the Steelers' Super Bowl plans, Troy recalls his quiet confidence rubbing off on players leading into the Super Bowl. He focused more on the football X's and O's, touting the Patriots' ability to be the more physical team. He tweaked the game plan, especially defensively, and simplified it in many ways. The message was simple: We're going to hit them, whether they have the football or not.

Looking back, that's what stands out to Troy, the fury with which

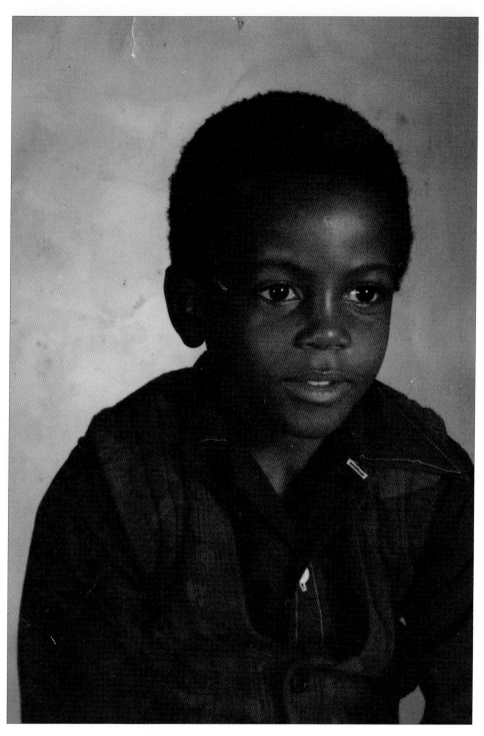

The steady gaze of a future special teamer. This is me in first grade.

Getting comfortable as a junior college player.

Breaking records at Marshall.

The first one will always be the sweetest. Here I am, running past Rams during our Super Bowl XXXVI victory. (AP Images/Tom DiPace)

And doing the same against the Panthers in Super Bowl XXXVIII, which we once again won on an Adam Vinatieri field goal. (AP Images/Tom DiPace)

Being chased by Eagles during our 24–21 victory in Super Bowl XXXIX.
(AP Images/David Drapkin)

And here I am announcing my retirement at Gillette Stadium on September 25, 2008. Bill Belichick and Bob Kraft said some really kind words about me that day, and the team even had "Troy Brown Night" during a Thursday night game on November 13, 2008. (AP Images/Robert E. Klein)

I had a chance to tell the fans how much I appreciated them when I was inducted into the Patriots Hall of Fame on September 16, 2012. (AP Images/Scott Boehm)

Me and Mom...

...and me and Dad with my sons, Sir'mon (standing) and SaanJay.

the defense hit.

Limiting the Rams to a 50-yard field goal in the first quarter was absolutely considered a victory, and with that, confidence among Troy and players only grew greater. Ty Law's 47-yard interception return for a touchdown and David Patten's eight-yard touchdown catch right before halftime—on a play similar to the AFC title game—staked the Patriots to a 14–3 lead.

The environment in the locker room was focused, as always. Players knew the game was far from over, and there would likely be some significant emotional swings in the second half.

That's exactly what unfolded, with Troy among those celebrating on the sideline when it looked like defensive back Tebucky Jones picked up a loose football and was racing almost the length of the field for a touchdown to add to the Patriots' lead and potentially close out the Rams. But a penalty nullified the play.

Soon enough, the Patriots were just holding on—a 17–3 lead sliced to 17–10 early in the fourth quarter, and then with less than two minutes remaining, the game was tied at 17. The Rams were gaining momentum, the Patriots were tiring, and personnel changes in the secondary were needed due to injuries.

As Troy stood on the sidelines, he thought to himself, "We can't let this one slip away. We have to find a way to outlast them."

He hoped to do his part on the ensuing kickoff, providing the offense good field position for a potential game-winning drive after the Rams had tied things up with 1:30 remaining. Television broadcaster John Madden said the Patriots would be smart to kneel and play for overtime.

What was going through Troy's mind at that moment? First, he thought back to the 1996 season and how he had missed the Super Bowl because of injury. Then he thought of how he longed to one day return to the game and play in it. And now that he was here, he so badly wanted to win it.

As much as he would have liked to have been the hero, as he was the week before in the AFC title game, Troy's kickoff return wasn't his best, only advancing to the 19-yard line.

While Madden debated on the television broadcast if the Patriots would be smarter to take a knee, Troy had a sense that the Patriots were thinking otherwise. The Rams had seized the momentum, and if the Patriots played for overtime, they were likely toast if they lost the coin toss.

Troy and his teammates had practiced situations like this and one of the things they always talked about was getting off to a good start. If it's a run, make sure it's not a negative play. If it's a pass, make sure it's completed, even if just for a few yards. Running back J.R. Redmond came through in that area, and Troy remembers being surprised that the Rams seemed to switch up their defense on that drive, playing more zone.

Troy himself took advantage of that with a 23-yard catch over the middle, something he didn't think would have been possible if not for the Rams' reliance on zone coverage. A key part of that play, Bill Belichick would later say, was Troy's presence of mind to get out of bounds and stop the clock because the Patriots were out of timeouts. That set the stage for Adam Vinatieri's game-winning 48-yard field goal.

As Vinatieri was lining up the kick, Troy simply didn't want to watch it. He took a seat on the bench, said a prayer, and held hands with a bunch of his teammates.

The next thing he heard was…nothing.

The crowd went silent, but still he couldn't peek. He clenched his hands that much tighter and then there was elation, the crowd roaring, and red, white, and blue confetti falling from above.

It all happened so fast, yet at the same time it felt like an eternity.

Troy joined his teammates in celebration, looking for anyone to hug and congratulate. Then he took the stage as a world champion.

How about that? Troy Brown, who was held back from playing football as a first grader because he was too small, was a world champion. He would later hear Tom Brady talk about how his favorite ring was the next one, but Troy always felt like nothing could top the first, especially after everything the Patriots went through that year.

Hearts were heavy because of the death of quarterback coach Dick Rehbein. There was Drew Bledsoe's injury in Week 2, a game played after the September 11 terrorist attacks. Then there was Tom Brady getting hurt in the AFC title game, with Bledsoe holding down the fort, followed by questions of whether it would be Brady or Bledsoe in the Super Bowl against one of the greatest teams of all-time.

For Troy, there was a lot of personal satisfaction in coming through on football's grandest stage. He finished with a team-high six catches for 89 yards in the game, and the 23-yarder to set up the game-winning field goal was one of the biggest plays of his career.

As it turned out, 2001 was his best year in the NFL—a career-high 101 catches, 1,199 yards, and five touchdowns. He was also the team's top punt returner (not to mention the NFL's leader in that category), taking two back for touchdowns.

Even sweeter was that his contributions were recognized across the NFL with a berth to the Pro Bowl.

At that point in his career, Troy had seen a little bit of everything. He had lived on the roster bubble as a rookie, got cut as a second-year player and wondered if he'd ever play again, earned some more security and opportunity upon his return, had the devastation of missing the Super Bowl because of injury, then saw what life was like when the culture of a team changes and not enough experienced, quality football players were imported.

Without question, 2001 was easily his favorite season. There was universal love for his teammates and respect for his coaches. Was it the most talented team? Troy always believed in himself, but at the same time, he's one of the first to say that '01 team didn't have the greatest offensive weapons. It started with the power running of Antowain Smith, and then there was Troy and David Patten at receiver, with J.R. Redmond and Kevin Faulk the third-down type backs, with some contributions from Patrick Pass as well.

Thankfully most everyone stayed healthy, because depth wasn't a strength. Everyone who did play executed their roles well and that personifies what a team is all about. Even as Troy was leading the team in catches, he still did his part on special teams, and he wasn't alone. Top defensive backs Ty Law and Lawyer Milloy were also part of special teams units, which are often viewed unfavorably by star players.

That was the mentality of that 2001 team: No one was bigger than the unsung job that needed to be done.

For Troy personally, it was the season he had been waiting for his entire career.

Eight

LIFE AT THE TOP
ISN'T EASY

It was bad football and Belichick said afterward,
"We just need to start over. There's
not much to work from."

CHAPTER EIGHT

Life at the Top Isn't Easy

Troy had been an underdog his entire life and the 2002 season was his first experience of living life at the top. He was a champion and everyone was now shooting to knock the Patriots off their perch atop the NFL mountain.

The Patriots had what Troy remembers as an excellent training camp that year, and the regular season couldn't have started much better. The season opener against the Pittsburgh Steelers, which also marked the opening of the team's sparkling new Gillette Stadium, was a rousing success.

New England recorded a 30–14 victory in that game, a rematch of the AFC Championship from Pittsburgh. At the time, some were questioning if the Patriots were a fluke team that just rode a hot streak to their Super Bowl title. But after quarterback Tom Brady threw for 294 yards and three touchdowns, it was a decisive statement.

Three new additions to the team's offense—tight end Christian Fauria and receivers Donald Hayes and Deion Branch—had touchdowns. That was a reflection of how the offense was well-rounded and featured more diverse options in the passing game. Brady himself was also growing. Considered more of a game manager in 2001, he threw 25 straight times during a stretch between the second and third quarters as the club turned a 10–7 lead into a 30–7 edge with an explosive stretch of football.

"We got whipped," Steelers receiver Plaxico Burress said after the game.

When the Patriots followed with a blowout 44–7 victory over the rival New York Jets on the road in Week 2, there was every reason for Troy and his teammates to feel good about themselves.

The Jets had opened that season with a 37–31 overtime win over the Buffalo Bills, and of course, one of the big story lines that week was how the Patriots and Jets were once again meeting in Week 2 of the season—one full year after the Week 2 game of 2001 in which Mo Lewis knocked out Drew Bledsoe.

The Patriots still had some doubters at that point, those wondering how good they really were.

"They're a great team," Jets cornerback Donnie Abraham told anyone who would listen after the blowout. "I think people have to start giving them credit. They don't look like they're feeling the pressure of being the defending Super Bowl champions. To me, it looks like they're having fun defending their title."

They were, and for Troy individually, the next week marked the best statistical performance of his career. The Kansas City Chiefs were in town and Troy finished with 16 receptions for 176 yards and a touchdown as the team recorded a 41–38 victory. It was one of those days where Troy felt like he was in the zone that athletes often talk about, and the synergy between him and quarterback Tom Brady was hard to miss. The ironic part about it is that Troy had a dropped pass early that could have set the tone for his day. Instead, he showed the mental toughness to fight through it and deliver.

But while many in the media were highlighting how the Patriots recorded a scintillating victory and Troy had a career day, a few things happened that day that were unfortunate.

First, Troy took a hit to the knee that he later pinpointed as one that affected him the rest of his career, and helped contribute to ending his career after the 2007 season. Second, the Chiefs exposed some chinks in the Patriots' armor—specifically on defense, as running back Priest Holmes rushed for 180 yards—and others around the NFL saw that on film and began to exploit them as well. That was a reminder of how a team can be 3–0, and everything might look good, but trouble can always be brewing behind the scenes. The football season is more marathon than sprint.

That probably best explains why Bill Belichick never seems to allow himself to get too high or too low during a season. There are so many ups and downs and that's what he preaches to players—to keep an even keel and get to work. He delivers that message in good times and bad times.

Bad times were ahead with a stretch of four straight losses—at San Diego (21–14), at Miami (26–13), vs. Green Bay (28–10), and vs. Denver (24–16).

Just like that, the defending champion Patriots went from 3–0 to 3–4.

Troy was leading the NFL in receptions after Week 3, but he had missed the San Diego and Miami games with the knee injury. He returned for the game against Green Bay, and if he needed a reminder of how fast things can change, he and his teammates heard boos from the home crowd during that loss. One of the lowlights was a slip screen that went wrong, resulting in a fumble, and only one Patriots player—offensive lineman Stephen Neal—went after the football.

It was bad football and Belichick said afterward, "We just need to start over. There's not much to work from."

Adding to the sting of defeat was that the game marked the return of former Patriots receiver Terry Glenn to town as a member of the Packers. He got the last laugh that day.

Troy offered no excuses, but looking back, he wondered if all the changes around the team—specifically playing in a nice new stadium—had players feeling more comfortable than they should have been. There was also, he thought, a feeling that maybe some around the team were starting to believe their press clippings of defending champions while forgetting what got them to that point.

For example, in a captains meeting, it was brought up that maybe the team could wear all-blue uniforms for a game. Oh, Belichick let the team have it for that one. When the Patriots lost in their all blue uniforms, Troy remembers he zinged the captains for focusing on the wrong things. The message was, in essence, "Don't worry what you look like, worry more about the way you're playing because it stinks!"

Troy knew it, and he also knew that his injured knee was hindering him from playing the way he wanted. He felt he came back from the injury a few games too early. He still ended up with a team-high 97 catches for 890 yards and three touchdowns, but he knew it could have been much better if he felt like he could run routes the way he wanted. He never found that zone again like he had against Kansas City before taking that hit on his knee.

In the end, the rest of the season felt like one big struggle; the weight of defending a championship too heavy for the team to bear. They played good football in spurts, and had a chance to sneak into the playoffs after winning five games in a six-game span from November 3 to December 8, but the bottom basically fell out with back-to-back losses to Tennessee (24–7) and the rival Jets (30–17) in mid-December.

The Patriots won their final game of the regular season, a 27–24 overtime decision over the Dolphins at home, and then Troy and his teammates went to the "Funway" on Rte. 1—the road leading to Gillette Stadium—to watch TV and see if they could back into the playoffs based on the result of the Jets-Packers game. For that stretch of time, the Patriots turned into Packers fans, but left disappointed when quarterback Brett Favre basically imploded.

That was a good lesson for Troy and his teammates. Leave your business unsettled for someone else to handle and that's what can happen. So one year after winning the Super Bowl in surprising fashion, and then silencing doubters with a strong start to the 2002 season, the Patriots didn't even qualify for the playoffs.

That's how fast things can change in the NFL. It was a hard fall from the top.

Nine

"BINGO! I'VE GOT BINGO!"

This was one of those moments for Troy where he had to submerge his personal feelings and put the team first.

CHAPTER NINE

"Bingo! I've Got Bingo!"

"Bill, he poked me in the eye! Come on, man!"

Troy was fired up during a training camp practice leading into the 2003 season, and while he wasn't known to raise his voice, the play of safety Rodney Harrison had officially drawn his ire. Harrison, after nine terrific seasons with the San Diego Chargers, had signed a free-agent contract with the Patriots and he was flying all over the place in practice.

The intensity, in one respect, was a good thing because it set the tone for the team. He was an instigator of sorts, sparking fights at times, like the time he found himself on the bottom of a pile with Troy and somehow his finger made his way into Troy's helmet. It likely wasn't intentional, but given the way Harrison was always pushing the envelope, Troy was hot and picked up the football and fired it at him.

Belichick, as Troy remembers it, showed little sympathy.

"Get back in the huddle, Troy. This is football!" he barked.

When emotions settled down, Troy realized this type of edge was probably a good thing for the team. With Harrison teaming up with Lawyer Milloy at safety, it was a hard-hitting combination, although there was a lingering question as to whether they were both in the long-term plans. That's because Troy and others knew about some behind-the-scenes battles Milloy was having with team management regarding his contract.

The Patriots wanted Milloy to take a pay cut, Milloy was resisting, and it was a stalemate. Troy never thought Milloy would simply be cut, especially since they had made it to the end of the preseason and the regular season was on the horizon. But that's what happened and it sent shockwaves through the locker room.

Troy remembers Milloy being there on Sunday, and just like that, it was Monday and he was gone. It was a stunning turn of events that sent reverberations through the locker room. Milloy, while sometimes coming on strong, was extremely well liked by Troy and others. Part of the reason for that is that Milloy always let you know where you stood with him. No sugarcoating it. So there was a lot of disappointment from players to see that happen to not only a captain, but a friend.

Even worse, Milloy was signed by the Buffalo Bills, who were hosting the Patriots in the first game of that 2003 season.

Bills 31, Patriots 0.

That was one of those days when the Bills, led by Milloy and quarterback Drew Bledsoe, were flying high on emotion. The Patriots, meanwhile, were flat and uninspired. When burly defensive lineman Sam Adams returned an interception 37 yards for a touchdown, it further highlighted a nightmare of a day for the Patriots and even former Patriots fullback Sam Gash was on the Buffalo team that year, which made it hurt that much more.

"It feels good, but in a positive way, not in a personal vendetta way," Milloy said after the game. "I could be sitting up here and throwing out names and sticking it to them, but they know."

Troy was embarrassed with the Patriots' performance, but at the same time, a small part of him was actually happy for Bledsoe, Milloy, and Gash. He also remembers the vital role that Harrison played in helping keep the defense together that year.

There was a lot of outside noise, specifically from ESPN and analyst Tom Jackson, who had talked about how players in New England "hate their coach." For Troy, hate was too strong of a word, but what that experience did for him was prepare him for his own ending. To see that happen to good friends Drew Bledsoe (traded) and Lawyer Milloy (released) was a cold-hearted reminder that it could happen to him too.

It's not personal, he reminded himself. Just business in a sport where there aren't guaranteed contracts.

Troy summed up his emotions this way: not mad, just disappointed. The disappointment was rooted in strong personal feelings for his friends, but also because it was hard to see how the decision made the Patriots a better football team. There was also a part of him that felt bad for Milloy, because Buffalo didn't seem like a great fit for him off the field.

A defining point of the 2003 season came in Week 2, with the Patriots traveling to face the Philadelphia Eagles. Emotions were still running high from the shocking release of Milloy, the Patriots had just been blown out, and facing quarterback Donovan McNabb and the Eagles wasn't viewed by many as an ideal spot to be.

Troy led the team with seven catches in the game, and it was a swarming defensive performance that produced six turnovers, seven sacks, and a convincing 31–10 triumph.

"Because we lost, there was the whole Lawyer issue," receiver David Patten said after the game. "We know we have a good team, we prepare well, and we have great coaches."

"It's not that complicated," added Belichick. "We played better, we executed better, we scored in the red [zone] and we played better defense in the red [zone]."

At the quarter mark of the season, the Patriots were 2–2. They wouldn't lose another game the rest of the year.

When Troy thinks back to 2003, and even the following year in 2004, one of the things that stands out was understanding the difference between being a good team and a great team. A big part of that was understanding that just because you're the defending champion, it doesn't ensure anything the following year. You have to start all over again with everyone else.

To Troy, 2003 had more of an all-business type feel to it. The locker-room chemistry was also very good; players hanging out and playing dominoes, trash-can basketball, and other fun games. In that sense, it was sort of a throwback feel to the mid-'90s and those Bill Parcells-coached teams. Yet when it was time to be in a meeting, or perform on the practice field, everything turned serious and players got to work. It was a perfect mix and the momentum built throughout the year.

A road game against the Dolphins on October 19 produced one of the most memorable plays of Troy's career—an 82-yard touchdown reception in overtime to secure a 19–13 victory. They don't get much more dramatic than that, which prompted Belichick to toss his headset into the air in celebration.

Troy got behind the defense, and Brady hit him in stride on "130 Gap Slant," the play helping the Patriots record their first win in their last six trips to Miami, which had long been a tough place for the team to win. Prior to that game, the Patriots had no wins in their 13 trips to Miami when games were played in September and October.

"It was unbelievable," Brady said afterward. "We were down and out a few times. The offensive line gave me a lot of time. I let it go and he made a great catch."

The 82-yarder was the longest catch of Troy's NFL career—who said he couldn't go deep?—and it was only possible because the Dolphins had missed two field goals. Every team needs a little luck from time to time.

Two weeks later, the Patriots recorded a 30–26 victory at Denver that was highlighted by an unusual call by Belichick to take an intentional safety. When you are around the game as long as Troy was at that point, and those types of things start going in your favor, it can snowball and momentum can build.

Such was the case in that 2003 season.

Then two weeks after that scintillating win over the Broncos, another notable contest came against the Parcells-coached Cowboys team. That was a big deal because a Cowboys visit to New England was rare, and also because it was the first time Belichick was facing Parcells since Belichick split from the Jets to become the Patriots head coach.

Cameras watched every move between the coaches before the game, as Parcells hovered near midfield and Belichick didn't walk over his way. Then after the game, a 12–0 Patriots win, they shared a brief embrace.

"Bill congratulated me on the win and I told him I thought he had a good football team," Belichick said afterward. "I wished him luck, and I do."

Parcells also downplayed things.

"I'm about tired of talking about that kind of thing. The guy did a helluva job for me for a long time," Parcells said. "People in the media can try and drive a stake between us if they want to, but that's not going to happen on my point."

To Troy, these were the two head coaches who meant the most to his NFL career. He avoided getting caught up in the hype, which was easier to do because he was sidelined at the time with an ankle injury.

The injury, as well as the emergence of second-year receivers Deion Branch and David Givens, ultimately led to a statistical decline for Troy that season—40 catches for 472 yards and four touchdowns. He was still the primary punt returner (29 for 293 yards, 10.1 average).

But that was still one of his most enjoyable seasons, in part because of the camaraderie among players. The locker-room vibe was good and when he looked to each side of him, he saw a player he could learn from—on and off the field. Top players like Rodney Harrison and Mike Vrabel volunteered to be on the scout team, which reflected a general selflessness among the group.

Whereas Troy once wondered about Harrison's intensity in practice—"Hey coach, he's poking me in the eye!"—he soon came to appreciate every opportunity he had to go up against him because it meant a chance for him to get better by facing one of the NFL's best safeties, not to mention trash-talkers.

Some of the practice chatter between Harrison and Vrabel, directed at Brady and the offense, often made Troy chuckle. Sometimes they'd call out the play in advance, trying to mess with Brady. Sometimes it ended up with Brady and Harrison yelling at each other, their competitive juices boiling over, the language not fit for a family audience. Vrabel used to pile on, telling Brady to just go back in the huddle and stop throwing interceptions. Or other times he would simulate the snap count to try to get into Brady's head. That was some fun stuff. Practice was entertaining and Troy could tell it would drive Brady crazy. The Patriots' defense was a strength that year and they would sometimes toy with the offense in practice.

But everyone ultimately had the same goal, to get better and win games, and that's why the ribbing was mostly a good thing. There were a lot of characters on that team, and good guys, with Troy pointing to left tackle Matt Light as one of them; just a fun dude, very positive, and a pleasure to be around.

Troy came to respect Light for a number of reasons, starting with his intelligence and the way he played the game. He saw how some fans would be hard on him, especially when there were struggles against high-motor pass-rushers like Dwight Freeney, but he always viewed that as a thankless job. You could have 65 good plays and one bad one, and the bad one was what everyone would be talking about.

On top of that, as the two progressed through the mid-2000s as teammates, Troy knew that Light had Crohn's disease but that he never used that as an excuse. Watching him go through that experience, come back at a much lighter weight, and then work his way back into top form was inspiring. He never complained and was, in Troy's view, one of the unsung players on those championship teams. It doesn't get much more important than protecting Tom Brady's blindside.

Light also represented the fun that particular group of players had together, his playful personality epitomizing a group that mostly seemed to enjoy being around each other. To Troy, that felt different than 2002 when maybe some players forgot about that aspect of things, perhaps the weight of defending a Super Bowl title was too much to bear. Yes, professional sports are a business, but it's also a game. Don't forget to have some fun.

Obviously it's a lot more fun when you're winning, and that's all the Patriots did that year following their 2–2 start. Troy saw the locker-room mix as being the perfect complement between experienced veterans who knew what it took to win with talented young receivers such as Deion Branch and David Givens. To Troy, the great thing about Branch and Givens was that they weren't just talented players but they were team-first guys, always thinking about what was best for the team. Troy found them easy to get along with, which wasn't always the case with players who had been brought into the team's receivers room.

So Branch and Givens fit right in. They were smart. They knew their football. And most of all, they knew how to get open. That's something Bill Belichick often said; the job of the receiver is to get open and catch the ball. Those two did that, and had a humble approach. When veterans like Troy had them carry their pads after a training camp practice, they did it without saying a word. Troy hadn't seen much of that in some other younger receivers, who trended more toward being a diva and not show the same willingness to put in the work. Troy became close friends with Branch, their bond still strong.

Compare that to a few other younger receivers, such as Bethel Johnson—a second-round draft choice out of Texas A&M in 2003—and it was a noticeable difference. Chad Jackson, another second-round pick from 2006, was another receiver with whom it just didn't click.

Then go back to the Pete Carroll years, 1997 to 1999, and the atmosphere was just much different. There wasn't as much discipline in those years, or the same level of attention to detail. Players didn't police each other the same way; instead they were looking out for themselves. In this case, whenever there was a problem—and there inevitably are a few along the way—they were handled in-house and in a way that inspired confidence that everyone was ultimately pulling in the same direction.

So Troy had a great feeling about the 2003 locker room. From his experience, whenever a team had that type of chemistry, it usually resulted in some type of championship success. He thought back to his high school team and how players were willing to line up at different positions than the one they truly wanted. There was something similar at Marshall, and Troy still keeps in touch with several of his former teammates from that time.

Part of what Troy felt fostered that atmosphere was that it was a group of players who had played elsewhere and had a chip of sorts on their shoulder. Linebacker Mike Vrabel had been with the Steelers but wasn't re-signed. Rodney Harrison had a long run with the Chargers but was let go. Receiver David Patten's career didn't truly take off until he arrived in New England.

Meanwhile, Troy represented the underdog as an eighth-round pick, while Tom Brady was emerging as a go-to guy and everyone knows his story—199th overall pick; he's the ultimate underdog turned superstar.

Add it all up and Troy viewed it as a team that had mostly under-the-radar players who were all about business. Everyone accepted their role, with Troy in the group as he went from a No. 1 type option to more of a No. 3.

That can be hard for some players to accept, but what Troy ultimately realized is that it probably helped prolong his career by a few years.

Two weeks after the much-hyped Patriots/Cowboys game that featured the first matchup of Bill Belichick vs. Bill Parcells since Belichick's departure from the Jets, there was another big rivalry game. It's just that the players and everyone else involved didn't quite know it was a rivalry just yet.

The Colts had Peyton Manning, the No. 1 pick of the 1998 draft, and they were an old AFC East rival who had been moved to the AFC South as part of the NFL's 2002 realignment into eight divisions of four teams each. At that point, Manning and Tom Brady were in the early stages of a budding back-and-forth rivalry and the November 30 game between the teams in Indianapolis that season was highly anticipated.

The Patriots' 38–34 win that day, when outside linebacker Willie

McGinest tackled running back Edgerrin James in the backfield on fourth-and-goal from the 1-yard line with 14 seconds remaining, might as well be viewed as the official beginning of the NFL's version of what Larry Bird vs. Magic Johnson was to the NBA in the 1980s.

From Troy's view, that was the time that both quarterbacks started to come of age. There was mutual respect between the two, and for the most part, the teams themselves.

The person who sparked some animosity for Patriots players was Colts president Bill Polian, who irritated players such as Troy by seemingly using his influence on the NFL's competition committee to change playing rules that the Patriots had used to their benefit. One example was the Patriots' physical defensive play and how Polian later helped enforce a change that provided more of an advantage to receivers.

Patriots defenders used to have a saying back then, "Have them in the water cooler." What that meant is that they hoped to knock down Colts receivers such as Marvin Harrison, push them into the bench and well…have them in the water cooler. The Colts had those pristine white uniforms and the Patriots wanted to have them dirtied by the end of a game.

Troy remembers how the weeks leading up to Colts games were some of the most gut-wrenching of all, players and coaches on edge. That was due, in part, to the respect that players had for Manning and how he could challenge them in ways most others at the position couldn't. With the Colts also improving on defense, they were one of the toughest teams the Patriots had to play. Tom Brady used to refer to pass-rushing defensive end Dwight Freeney as the one player he'd have nightmares about because of his quickness from the blindside.

In that wild November 30 game, the Patriots jumped out to a 31–10 lead midway through the third quarter before Manning came roaring back. It looked like it was going to be a devastating loss at the end before McGinest's heroics. McGinest had limped off the field a few plays earlier, which annoyed some Colts players who felt he was embellishing.

"When it came down to it for the gusto, our guys came with it on the goal-line," McGinest said. "That's how you want to win it."

Prior to the play, fellow linebacker Ted Johnson figured the team's seven-game winning streak was going to be snapped.

"I was thinking, 'It's looking pretty bleak,'" he said afterward. "But are you surprised? With this team?"

At that point, Troy felt the Patriots had a little bit of a mental edge over Manning and the Colts. Sure, they had great appreciation for his skills, but they also felt that if it was a close game coming down to the end that Manning and Co. would struggle to get over the hump. The Patriots, from Troy's view, felt they could get in Manning's head and dictate the way the game was played. The Patriots always wanted to be physical, they often disguised intentions before the snap, and the goal was to keep everyone guessing.

The teams not only met up in late November that season, but also in the AFC Championship Game just seven weeks later. By that point, the Patriots had won 13 straight, narrowly escaping an upset in the divisional round against the Tennessee Titans in one of the coldest games in franchise history.

It was another chilly game against the Colts, and the defense once again flummoxed Manning, with Troy's close friend, Ty Law, intercepting him three times. The Patriots built a 15–0 lead in the first half, and in the end, five Adam Vinatieri field goals were critical in a 24–14 victory.

Troy finished with seven catches for a team-high 88 yards in helping clinch a Super Bowl berth, his third as a player. He missed the first one, in 1996, due to injury. He played a pivotal role in the second one, in 2001, as the team's leading receiver. In this one, he was in store for a surprise just two days before the game.

As Troy settled in for dinner on Friday night, receivers coach Brian Daboll approached him and told him that instead of being the No. 3 receiver and playing mostly in the slot, the coaches wanted him to start and play the "Z" position in two-receiver sets. That was the spot David Givens had been playing, and while Troy would do anything to help the team, his first reaction was along the lines of "Are you serious?"

That was partially because he had not taken any practice reps at the position, a result of Deion Branch and Givens being the primary outside receivers. In one respect, Troy viewed it as a nod from the coaching staff that they wanted him to be in that position in the most important game of the season. In another respect, he felt awful for Givens, who he knew would take the news hard.

So Troy, in his role as a team leader, had a heart-to-heart talk with him. He told him not to get down and that the team would need him in the game, and it was important to stay mentally focused. Troy's leadership in that moment, coupled with Givens' ability to rise above it, was a critical behind-the-scenes moment that year.

Givens ended up with five catches for 69 yards and one touchdown in the Super Bowl, while Troy had eight receptions for 76 yards. Branch was the most productive receiver, totaling 10 catches for 143 yards and a touchdown.

The Patriots got a lot from their receiving corps in the game and when Bill Belichick reflected on Troy's contributions, he remembered how when the game was tied at 29 and New England was driving for the game-winning field goal, it was Troy coming up with a few huge catches. One of them, a 13-yarder on first-and-20, was one of the most important plays of all because it helped dig the offense out of a tough spot after Troy himself was called for offensive pass interference on the play before.

Then on third-and-3, Troy figured the ball might be coming his way again, just the way it had in the Super Bowl win over the Rams to set up the game-winning field goal. But this time, the ball was going to Deion Branch.

This was one of those moments for Troy where he had to submerge his personal feelings and put the team first. He felt strongly that he was the best option for the team at that moment, and it was a thought that was hard for him to clear out of his head as he broke the huddle and aligned incorrectly. It wasn't that Troy didn't know where to line up; it was just that he was taken aback by not being the primary option.

Looking back, that was probably the moment that Troy realized that his role with the team wasn't what it once was. He felt that at times over the course of the regular season, of course, but it took a moment like the Super Bowl to really have it hit home like that. He then thought of his close friend Drew Bledsoe, and how he gracefully handled having his role forever altered by Tom Brady's emergence, before realizing there was only one way to proceed—put his head down and do whatever the team needed.

So on the play that Branch gained 17 yards with 14 seconds remaining, setting up Adam Vinatieri's game-winning 41-yard field goal, Troy ran as good a route as he could, knowing that if Branch wasn't open he might be a second option. He was open. But so was Branch.

That turn of events caught him a bit off guard, forcing him to accept that things were changing for him in terms of his role on the team. At the same time, he was a Super Bowl champion once again, and his contributions—while not showing up as much on the stat sheet—were still very meaningful.

In the parade following that Super Bowl, Troy delivered a humorous line that remained with him throughout the rest of his career. "Bingo! I've got bingo!"

Those words played off a television commercial he had been a part of that year, through the NFL and United Way. In the commercial, Troy's competitive nature was highlighted as he "competed" with senior citizens in horseshoes, archery, racquetball, shuffleboard, and bingo—dominating each time and celebrating in the process.

The senior citizens grew tired of Troy's act and put a pie on his seat after he stood up following another bingo win, surprising him as he sat down.

So during the celebratory Super Bowl parade, Troy let everyone know that once again he had bingo. What he later discovered is that to get back to the same point again next year, he'd be forced to do things on the football field that few could have predicted.

Ten

"DEFENSE? YOU WANT ME TO PLAY DEFENSE?"

Troy vividly remembers Charlie Weis, the team's offensive coordinator with the sharp tongue, saying that it was a good thing the one-day experiment was over so he could get back to using him on offense.

CHAPTER TEN

"Defense? You Want Me to Play Defense?"

"Defense? You want me to play defense?"

Troy knew he was in the twilight years at this point, the 2004 season, having first entered the NFL in 1993. The Patriots were coming off that amazing '03 Super Bowl season that concluded with 15 straight victories and even though every team has to start all over again, Troy felt a certain momentum carry over to the next training camp.

But for him personally, it was probably the most unique year of his career. It started in training camp when the team's defensive coordinator, Eric Mangini, handed him some notes for practice, highlighting certain areas for emphasis.

"Why is Mangini coming up to me?" Troy asked.

The answer, of course, was because Bill Belichick and the coaching staff wanted to cross-train him on defense just in case there was an emergency over the course of the season. The coaching staff saw a deep receiving corps with Deion Branch, David Givens and David Patten, and true to the saying "the more you can do, the more valuable you are to the team," they wanted to see how Troy looked playing cornerback.

Troy tried to view it as a compliment, the idea that Belichick trusted him not to screw it up. He also knew he was an older player on the roster and this was a way he could possibly secure a roster spot. Times sure were different for him, taking him back to his college career at Marshall when he played some defensive back.

As players walk to practice during training camp, there is some time for them to mentally get themselves in a good place because of the distance of the fields from the locker room. There is also a set of stairs for them to climb, and that first day he was to practice on defense, Troy remembers the walk as if it were a marathon. It took forever.

What happened over the next couple of hours was Troy's indoctrination to defense and he remembers it wasn't always pretty. With thousands of fans in attendance, he had a tough day. Troy vividly remembers Charlie Weis, the team's offensive coordinator with the sharp tongue, saying that it was a good thing the one-day experiment was over so he could get back to using him on offense.

Weis' ire was raised the next day when Troy was still part of defensive meetings. Coaches didn't expect an instant success story and stuck with it, which would pay off down the road.

With each practice, Troy got better and better, and his confidence grew. What he learned was that he actually might have an advantage as a cornerback because he had the mind of a receiver. So he'd ask himself questions before the snap and as the play unfolded.

"If I was a receiver in this situation, what would I be thinking?"

"Is he going to pick me here?"

"The way he's aligned, so close to the tight end, do I need to back off?"

Troy's teammates also helped, telling him to look for certain things that could help him, and he worked himself to the point that if the call came in the regular season he felt like he would at least be able to be competitive. He was moving back to offense, of course, but knew that he was an emergency option on defense if needed.

The Patriots opened that season with six straight victories, which fueled the hype around the team because that upped the franchise's winning streak to 21 games (when counting the 2003 season). The season-opener was against Peyton Manning and the Indianapolis Colts, which added another chapter in that budding rivalry.

The Patriots won 27–24, and Troy was inactive because of injury. Troy's primary contributions would have come as the team's punt returner, which was a role that cornerback Tyrone Poole and receiver Deion Branch teamed up to handle, and when Branch muffed a punt in the fourth quarter and the Colts took over and drove to the 1, the Patriots looked vulnerable.

But Colts running back Edgerrin James fumbled at the 1-yard line with just less than four minutes remaining. The Patriots recovered and ultimately survived.

Troy was back in the lineup the following week in a 23–12 road win over the Arizona Cardinals. He caught one pass for six yards and took all four punt returns, which reflected his niche on the club. He would finish that season with just 17 catches for 184 yards, his lowest production since the 1995 season, his third in the NFL.

Troy had injured his shoulder in a 31–17 win over the Buffalo Bills in Week 3 of that season, which knocked him out of the next three games—victories over the Miami Dolphins (24–10), Seattle

Seahawks (30–20), and New York Jets (13–7).

He came back for a highly anticipated road game against the Pittsburgh Steelers on Halloween night. The Patriots and Steelers had developed a healthy rivalry at that point, highlighted by the AFC Championship Game following the 2001 regular season. Troy viewed that rivalry differently from the Colts, whose explosive offense could unnerve anyone. The Steelers were more of a big physical team, and in 2004 they had a rookie quarterback, Ben Roethlisberger out of Miami of Ohio, who fit that mold.

So this was a new chapter in the rivalry between the teams, even if the Steelers' defense looked the same with its focus on the zone-blitz scheme. For the Patriots' offense, the thought was always that if it could give quarterback Tom Brady time against the blitz, they would be able to move the ball and score points against a Pittsburgh secondary that was just okay. Meanwhile, Pittsburgh quarterback Kordell Stewart was an inexperienced passer who was prone to mistakes.

But this was Roethlisberger's team now, and nothing seemed to go right for the Patriots in that game against the Steelers. They lost 34–20 to have their 21-game win streak broken. The Steelers, meanwhile, were now the kings of the AFC as they had win six straight since Roethlisberger had taken over from the injured Tommy Maddox.

"They outplayed us and they outcoached us," Patriots coach Bill Belichick said afterward. "Pittsburgh played an outstanding game. It's what you expect when two opposing forces collide. We got beat. We got killed. When we turn the ball over and can't stop them on top of that, we're dead."

On top of that, the team's best cornerback Ty Law, injured his foot and wouldn't be available for action. Troy sensed what was coming the following week, some snaps in practice on defense as the team prepared for its next game—a road contest at the St. Louis Rams.

Still, the hope was that Troy wouldn't be needed during the game. Troy remembers coaches saying if the team could get to the third or fourth quarter, they thought they'd be okay.

The Patriots entered the game without both starting cornerbacks, Ty Law and Tyrone Poole, and then fill-in Asante Samuel banged up his shoulder and came screaming toward the sideline. As Troy heard Samuel in agony, he knew what was coming next: "Troy, get in there!"

"We moved guys around from different positions, but they just hung in there and kept fighting," Bill Belichick said after the game. "Those players really stepped up."

None more than Troy, who was playing alongside a former undrafted free agent, Randall Gay, and a player who had just been signed to a contract the prior Saturday, Earthwind Moreland.

As part of their defensive plan, the Patriots brought significant pressure on Rams quarterback Marc Bulger, hoping to disrupt the timing of the passing game and aid a patchwork secondary. Bulger was sacked five times, intercepted once, and the Patriots also forced a fumble.

"I probably held on to the ball too long sometimes," Bulger acknowledged.

As for Troy, the challenge couldn't have been much greater considering the Rams had players like Marshall Faulk, Isaac Bruce, Torry Holt, and Sean McDonald on their roster. McDonald had blazing speed and Troy remembers getting beaten badly by him down the field, only to be fortunate that Bulger didn't have the arm strength to reach him.

Because of performances like Troy's, Belichick called the game "probably as complete a victory as I've ever been around."

When Belichick talks like that, it's usually a result of big plays being produced in all three phases of the game—offense, defense, and special teams. One play, in particular, that he liked was a fake field goal in which kicker Adam Vinatieri found Troy for a four-yard touchdown in the third quarter. It was also a game where goal-line tight end Mike Vrabel—whose primary job was to play linebacker— had a touchdown catch.

On Troy's touchdown, he casually drifted to the outside and the Rams were slow to react.

"You kind of hope to get these guys sleeping a little bit and we did," Vinatieri said. "Troy kind of hid out on the side and we snapped the ball before they noticed him."

That irritated fiery Rams coach Mike Martz, who had tried to call a timeout.

"I don't think that was the trickiest thing in the world," he said. "Where was he going, to the john? We've got to pay more attention than that."

Troy's attention to detail helped him produce three interceptions that season, which tied for the second most on the team. His first one came against his close friend and former teammate, Buffalo Bills quarterback Drew Bledsoe, the week after his defensive debut (the Patriots crushed the Bills 29–6).

The interception came in the fourth quarter when he aligned in the slot.

"Eric Moulds, he's their go-to guy," Troy said that day. "I figured they'd be throwing it to him, so I was ready."

At that point, the Patriots had an 8–1 record and were going toe-to-toe in the standings with the Pittsburgh team they had lost to on Halloween for AFC supremacy. Troy picked up his second career interception in an early December game against Cleveland, this time picking off quarterback Luke McCown in a 42–15 win. Troy's assignment was to shadow slot receiver Dennis Northcutt.

"All I know is that I'm having a lot of fun right now," he said after the game. "I think the thing we always keep in mind as a team is that it doesn't matter what the score is, or what the team's record is we're playing. If you let your guard down, you're going to get beat. You have to play all-out all of the time. It's all mental toughness. It's hard to keep that up for an entire season and the teams that can do that are the teams who have a chance to win it all at the end."

That strong mental approach was something that had stood out to Troy early in that 2004 season, from the perspective of it permeating throughout the locker room. There was a lot of pressure on the team that season, a result of being the defending champions and having won 15 games in a row the year before and carrying that streak into the season.

In 2002, Troy felt the team didn't handle that type of pressure as well as it could have. This team was different.

When media coverage grew more intense early in 2004, Troy would take pride in saying that he didn't even know how many games the team had won in a row. That's because he was just focused on the next game, which is the one-game-at-a-time mantra Belichick would always preach. From his experience, Troy knew that the quicker players adopted that line of thinking, the better chance they had to win a title.

To emphasize that point, Rodney Harrison, the team's hard-hitting safety, would often say that the team was just trying to improve to 1–0 each week. So by treating each opponent with respect, the Patriots never seemed to get too far ahead of themselves that year. Troy felt that was a reflection of the collection of players who were physically and mentally tough, and also shined in "situational football." Every situation that came up in a game, they usually delivered. Confidence was gained on a weekly basis when the team would practice certain situations, then they would come up in games. To Troy, that helped everyone play faster in the actual games.

An example of this came in the season-opener against the Colts.

Indianapolis was driving for either a game-winning touchdown or game-tying field goal with less than two minutes remaining, and it was third-and-8 from the Patriots' 17-yard line. At a time when it looked like Peyton Manning was finally going to rewrite the storyline of not being able to overcome Bill Belichick and the Patriots, outside linebacker Willie McGinest burst through and sacked him 12 yards behind the line of scrimmage, changing field position. What would have been a 36-yard field goal became a 48-yarder and kicker Mike Vanderjagt, who had rubbed his fingers together before the kick to indicate that he was money, missed it. Vanderjagt had made 42 field goals in a row before that kick.

Troy's final interception that season came in a 35–28 home victory over the Bengals on December 12. Cincinnati was driving deep in Patriots territory early in the fourth quarter when backup quarterback Jon Kitna, who had entered the game for the injured Carson Palmer (knee), tried to fit the ball into a tight window to receiver Chad Johnson in the end zone. Brown stepped in front of it to make the interception.

"I should have caught it and gone down, but my offensive mentality took over," Troy said. "When you get the ball in your hands, run with it."

One thing the Patriots were doing well as a team was setting the tone by scoring first. The win over the Bengals, which players felt good about because it came against running back Corey Dillon's former team, was the 18th game in a row that New England had scored first. So even with players like Troy taking on new roles, they were finding a way to play games on their terms.

The only time things caught up to them was in a late December game at Miami, where the Dolphins entered with a 2–11 record and faced an uncertain future as they were playing under interim coach Jim Bates, who had taken over after Dave Wannstedt resigned weeks earlier. Miami rallied from an 11-point deficit with 3:59 remaining and scored the game-winning touchdown when receiver Derrius Thompson caught a 21-yard touchdown pass on fourth-and-10 with 1:23 remaining.

Troy was the player in coverage.

"We wanted to get some matchups on Troy," Bates explained. "He had three interceptions coming in, but it's tough to go over and play defensive back. Derrius made a great catch."

Troy felt as if he had cost the Patriots the game, but he quickly learned an important lesson: When playing cornerback, you're often out on an island, and you quickly need to move on to the next play. Support from teammates like Tedy Bruschi and Rodney Harrison helped him greatly.

That was something Troy noticed Tom Brady did a great job of as the team's quarterback. In the loss to Miami, Brady had also made a costly miscue, throwing an interception from his backside.

The Patriots finished the season with victories over the New York Jets (23–7) and San Francisco 49ers (21–7), which set up another date with the rival Colts in the AFC divisional round at the Patriots' home stadium in Foxborough. But privately, Troy was struggling.

The pressure of playing defense was mounting, and he often felt like he stood out because there were no other players with the jersey No. 80 on that side of the ball. He felt like he had a bulls-eye on his back at times, and to no one's surprise, Bill Belichick still demanded a lot despite his inexperience. For example, there were some complex blitz schemes that required Troy to communicate and sometimes make a call that helped every other defensive player get on the same page.

This is often what fans don't see, both on the field and off the field, how the pressure to handle those situations can be a burden. Troy put a lot of pressure on himself. He started to lose sleep, running through the various scenarios in his mind.

He would ask himself a series of questions: How do I react? What if the offense shifts? How do I handle a player coming in motion to my side? What if the personnel on offense changes?

For a player to perform to his capabilities, confidence needs to be at a high level and Troy's was waning. He started to worry about himself and so did teammates like Rodney Harrison, who remembers expressing concern to Belichick about Troy's situation.

In the divisional round of the playoffs, the Patriots defeated Peyton Manning and the Indianapolis Colts 20–3. Troy mostly covered slot receiver Brandon Stokley, who finished with eight catches for 64 yards. The result improved Tom Brady to 7–0 in the playoffs at the time, while Manning was 0–7 in games played in Foxborough.

Harrison called it the greatest game plan he'd ever seen, as the Patriots held a 37:43 to 22:17 time-of-possession edge. For Troy, it was a typical game of doing a little bit of everything; he had two receptions as a starter on offense, two punt returns, and three tackles on defense.

It was more of the same for Troy the next week in the AFC Championship Game against the Pittsburgh Steelers as he continued to contribute on offense (1 catch for 11 yards), defense (3 tackles) and special teams (2 punt returns). For the Patriots to victoriously return to Pittsburgh, where they had won the AFC title game in 2001 but had also lost a regular season game in 2004 to snap their 21-game win streak, was sweet for players.

Now Troy was going back to the Super Bowl, this time against the Philadelphia Eagles in Jacksonville, Florida.

To some, Troy represented the unselfish personality of the entire Patriots team that year. At age 33, he had embraced a new position on defense, and his position switch was a topical storyline leading into the Super Bowl.

"I wasn't afraid," Troy recalled that week. "I was more nervous than anything else. I knew I had the ability, but I had to believe myself that I could go out there and get it done. My first game, a team like the Rams, that part was scary."

The Super Bowl was also a week where Bill Belichick used remarks made by Eagles receiver Freddie Mitchell as motivation for Patriots players. Mitchell had said he didn't even know the names of the players in the Patriots' patchwork secondary, just their numbers. That riled up Belichick, who seemed to take pride in defending players like Troy.

What Belichick seemed to respect most was that as Troy's role on offense was diminishing, he found a way to carve out a different niche on the club.

"You don't just get handed a job," he said.

No, to become a franchise Hall of Famer, you have to work hard for it. That was the Troy Brown way.

"What I do best is go out there, make plays, and try to set a good example for this football team," Troy said leading into the Super Bowl. "The best way to be a champion is to be unselfish and do whatever is asked of you to help your team. That is what I am all about."

The Patriots went on to beat the Eagles 24–21.

Troy had bingo again.

Eleven

NEARLY A SAINT

Sometimes a rivalry can turn, and Troy
remembers that as the night it did for the Colts.

CHAPTER ELEVEN

Nearly a Saint

In the aftermath of the Patriots' Super Bowl victory over the Eagles, as players celebrated on the field, some held up copies of the team's official newspaper *Patriots Football Weekly* that declared them a dynasty. To win three Super Bowls in a span of four years was unprecedented in the salary-cap era, and as players returned in 2005, they set the lofty goal of trying to win three straight championships. No franchise had ever accomplished the feat.

Troy felt that the core of the team had learned a lot of valuable lessons over those four seasons. Mainly, it was how to deal with success and keep raising the bar. That can be challenging as a player. When you win, everyone wants a piece of you. There are more marketing opportunities and the media spotlight shines brighter. If a player isn't disciplined enough, that can distract from the most important business of all—the business of football.

For Troy and others, it was hard not to notice all the change around them. The team's two coordinators, Charlie Weis on offense and Romeo Crennel on defense, moved on to head-coaching jobs. Weis landed at Notre Dame and Crennel went to the NFL's Cleveland Browns.

Meanwhile, in the locker room, cornerback Ty Law, receiver David Patten, and linebackers Roman Phifer and Ted Johnson were among those who were no longer with the team. And with linebacker Tedy Bruschi recovering from a stroke, he wasn't around the team either.

Troy himself almost wasn't around. In February, he was released in a salary-cap move as the team elected not to pay a $2.5 million roster bonus and his $2.5 million base salary. The move saved the team about $5 million on the salary cap. Troy was 33 at the time.

"There's always a chance that he could return," Brown's agent, Gary Uberstine, said at the time. "Neither side is burning bridges."

The New Orleans Saints made a strong push to sign him, but Troy wanted to stay in New England and ultimately decided to stick around even though he potentially could have made more money in New Orleans. The offer from the Patriots, who always wanted to retain Troy, just at a lower salary, was for the veteran minimum. One aspect that complicated the decision for Troy was the presence of Chris Scelfo, an assistant coach at Marshall when he played there, as Tulane's head coach.

The idea of playing in New Orleans, and being closer to Scelfo, was appealing to Troy. Jim Haslett was the Saints' coach at the time and Troy recalls that he was pretty close to signing with New Orleans. But in the end, he set any hard feelings aside, considered where he was at that point in his career, and decided to stay with the Patriots because it was the best thing for his family at that point.

Looking back at that time, Troy felt it was the right decision. Part of the reason was that was the year in which Hurricane Katrina devastated New Orleans. At the time, Katrina was the largest and third strongest hurricane ever recorded to make landfall in the United States. It peaked as a Category 5 hurricane with winds up to 175 miles per hour, and thousands of lives were lost.

Furthermore, staying with the Patriots meant he wouldn't have to start all over again with a new offensive system. There was a level of comfort in New England that he appreciated. Once Troy made the decision to stay in New England, coach Bill Belichick lauded him as one of the team's foundation-type players.

"In this era, it's very unusual for a player to remain with one team for as long as Troy's career as a Patriot," Belichick said. "Troy Brown is a special player and person and we are glad to have him back."

In addition to Troy, the Patriots also brought in speedy receiver Tim Dwight, who became the primary punt returner and was competition for repetitions at receiver behind Deion Branch and David Givens. Also, competition came in the form of former first-round draft pick David Terrell, who the team was hoping could flash some of the potential and form that made him a highly-touted prospect out of Michigan in 2001, the year in which the Patriots selected defensive lineman Richard Seymour with the sixth overall draft pick despite some in the media calling for Terrell to be the pick.

The team couldn't get in a rhythm early in the year. Things did start on a high note, with the team's championship banner being raised before a 30–20 season-opening victory over the Oakland Raiders.

The game had all the obvious story lines, as it provided a chance to consider how the two franchises had taken different paths since their meeting in the "Snow Bowl" divisional round playoff game following the 2001 season. The Raiders went to the Super Bowl the next season before falling on hard times (9–23 over the 2003–04 seasons), while the Patriots had their blip in 2002 before winning two more Super Bowls.

Troy himself was coming off a 2004 season in which he made his biggest mark on defense, pressed into duty as an emergency cornerback, but he was almost exclusively back on offense in 2005. After catching 17 passes in 2004, he had six in the opener against Oakland.

Quarterback Tom Brady threw for 306 yards and two touchdowns in the season opener, while a strong pass rush from defensive lineman Richard Seymour helped create a game-swinging turnover in the third quarter that tilted the momentum in the Patriots' favor. New England had some struggles with Oakland receiver Randy Moss, who had a 73-yard touchdown catch, which in a sense foreshadowed what would happen two years later—Moss coming back to Gillette Stadium to play for the Patriots and team up with Troy in his final season. The two had a natural connection from attending Marshall University, albeit at different times.

As for the Patriots' 2005 season, the up-and-down nature of it was reflected in the pattern that unfolded over the first eight games. After the opening win over Oakland, it went like this:

27–17 loss at Carolina

23–20 win at Pittsburgh

41–17 loss to San Diego

31–28 win at Atlanta

28–20 loss at Denver

21–16 win over Buffalo

40–21 loss to Indianapolis

Troy had a 71-yard catch in the Week 2 loss to Carolina to set up the team's first touchdown, showing he could still be productive in picking up yardage in chunks. He added four catches for 43 yards the next week against the Steelers, giving him 13 catches in the first three games. But Troy injured his big toe in Week 5 against Atlanta, which had him on the sidelines for the next two games.

What Troy remembers about that stretch was that it was a real grind, and he wasn't the only one who felt it. Playing a tough schedule as the defending champion, it was wearing on many in the locker room. The loss to the Chargers in Week 4 was especially disheartening because it snapped the team's 20-game winning streak at home and represented a significant chink in the team's armor. The Patriots had devoted a lot of attention to tight end Antonio Gates in the game and still couldn't stop him. Quarterback Drew Brees seemed like he was just throwing the ball up to Gates and the Patriots simply didn't have an answer.

So that was the first sign that this Patriots team had an uphill climb ahead of itself. Another sign of their struggle came in the loss to the Colts.

Troy had seen the Patriots have the Colts' number over the years, specifically since Peyton Manning became their quarterback as the No. 1 pick in the 1998 draft. Troy and the Patriots had always respected the Colts, and there were some memorable games between the teams, but the story line at the time was how Bill Belichick was in Manning's head. Manning entered the game with an 0–7 record in games played in Foxborough.

This turned out to be Manning's breakthrough, a 40–21 victory in which he threw three touchdown passes, Edgerrin James rushed for 104 yards, and receivers Marvin Harrison and Reggie Wayne each eclipsed 100 yards.

"We wanted to execute and get a lead on this team. We haven't had a lead on this team in a long time," Manning said. "The idea is to try to dictate to the defense."

That was Troy's first game returning from his toe injury and he finished with five catches for 57 yards, which included a 19-yard touchdown grab. But the Patriots dropped to 4–4 at the midpoint of the season and there seemed to be more questions than answers at the time.

Sometimes a rivalry can turn, and Troy remembers that as the night it did for the Colts. They had been knocked around for years by the Patriots, coming oh-so-close to getting that first win, and now they had their victory. Some said at the time that's when Patriots-Colts officially became a rivalry.

Troy thought the Patriots were real contenders entering that year, but at that point, he admits that there was a feeling the club wasn't as good as he thought it was; too much inconsistency. The defense really struggled, even as Tedy Bruschi miraculously returned from his stroke, and Troy couldn't quite figure out why the offense was having so much trouble because there was a lot of talent on that unit. It was what Troy refers to as a "scratch and claw" season where you try to grind it out and hope that maybe the team catches fire.

After that loss to the Colts, a 23–16 win at Miami helped spark a nice little run that saw the Patriots win six of their final eight games to finish the year 10–6. That was a dramatic game as the Patriots had fell behind 16–15 with just less than three minutes to play before a two-play drive produced the go-ahead touchdown before the defense closed things out.

"This is one of those great games that went back and forth," Belichick said of the first-ever coaching matchup against his former assistant with the Cleveland Browns, Nick Saban. "It turned into a track meet at the end. I'm proud of the guys for hanging in there."

The game was remembered for, among other things, former Dolphins fullback Heath Evans putting on a show as the Patriots' emergency lead ball-carrier after being thrust into the role because of a string of injuries to others. Troy had three catches for 36 yards.

The Patriots beat the team Troy almost signed with the next week, the Saints, but Troy didn't play as his toe injury was still lingering. He returned the following week and ended up finishing the regular season with 39 receptions for 466 yards and two touchdowns. That more than doubled his output from the prior year (17 catches, 184 yards) and after a grind of a season, he knew that the team had still accomplished its goal of making the playoffs. Once in, anything can happen. Troy knew this wasn't the same Patriots team of the past two years, but stranger things have happened.

Then the Patriots put together a thoroughly impressive 28–3 victory over the visiting Jacksonville Jaguars in the AFC wild-card round of the playoffs. Troy opened the scoring with an 11-yard touchdown catch, which was his one reception for the game. It was a 7–3 lead at halftime before the Patriots exploded in the second half with a performance that had Troy and his teammates confident heading into a road game against the Denver Broncos in the AFC divisional round.

The Patriots had lost at Denver earlier in the season and had heard plenty of chatter about how they couldn't win in the Mile High City. Two things stood out to Troy about that game, a 27–13 loss that officially ended the team's season: 1) Players who usually stepped up to make plays didn't come through; 2) Tight end Benjamin Watson's great hustle play to chase down cornerback Champ Bailey on a 100-yard interception return.

As for players not coming through, Troy was part of that as well, as he muffed a punt that the Broncos recovered and turned into a touchdown in the fourth quarter to go up 24–6.

Things had unraveled at that point, as the Patriots had been in the game late in the third quarter, trailing 10–6, and having advanced to the Broncos' 5-yard line. That's when quarterback Tom Brady attempted to throw to Troy in the end zone, and Bailey intercepted it and raced in the other direction. It looked like Bailey would dart the full 101 yards (he caught it one yard deep in the end zone), but Benjamin Watson's full-out hustle sprint helped him catch him at the 1-yard line. Watson knocked the ball out of Bailey's hands and, from the Patriots' view, it went through the end zone which should have resulted in a touchback. But officials ruled it out of bounds and gave the Broncos the ball at the 1, and they scored on the next play.

Replay reviews were inconclusive and that play has been the genesis for Belichick pushing the NFL to place fixed cameras at all boundary lines to ensure coaches and officials would have good angles on such replays.

Troy remembered the scene on the sidelines during that game

as not being pleasant, which was reflected in linebackers Willie McGinest and Larry Izzo getting into a shoving match. The frustration among players was mounting. To Troy, that wasn't the way the Patriots have generally operated and it somewhat epitomized that entire season. It was a struggle and very much unlike the prior two Super Bowl championship years. It was a difficult one.

The next one would be too, although Troy would put his name in the record book.

Twelve

ELATION AND DESPAIR
IN THE '06 PLAYOFFS

"He's the prototype Patriot—selfless, offense, defense, special teams. He never did fancy dances, just did what's right both on and off the field."

CHAPTER TWELVE

Elation and Despair in the '06 Playoffs

Entering 2006, Troy was in a year-to-year type mindset. If he played, he pretty much decided it would be with the Patriots and he understood it would likely be for a minimum-level contract. Troy decided to return for a 14th season, and specific to the wide receiver position, he had never really seen as many changes as unfolded that off-season.

Deion Branch, his close friend who had done great things since joining the team as a second-round draft choice in 2002, was traded to the Seattle Seahawks after a headline-grabbing contract stalemate.

David Givens, who had emerged from a 2002 seventh-round draft choice to key contributor, signed a lucrative free-agent deal with the Tennessee Titans.

Speedy veteran receiver Tim Dwight, who had been signed the year before, wasn't back.

Troy was essentially the lone holdover, which surprised him because he wasn't even a starter at that point. As unsettling as it was at times, Troy didn't have any gripes with Branch, who didn't report to camp, because that's the way business works. That can sometimes be misunderstood by those who follow a team; as much as players want to field the best team possible, everyone understands that there is a business side to the game. Troy had seen plenty of that over his 14 years in the NFL, so he played the dual role of trying to be the best teammate he could be, as well as the best friend possible to Branch.

Troy's situation was different at that point. It would have taken a mega-offer for him to leave the Patriots. He had already received his big paydays, and while an opportunity with the Saints was enticing the year before, he wanted to do everything possible to try to start and finish his career with the same team.

Compare that to Branch, who had his first chance to become a free agent in the off-season leading into the 2006 campaign. He wanted to cash in, because he might not have that chance again and he had some leverage as a former Super Bowl MVP who put up impressive numbers in his first four years in the league (213 receptions, 2,744 yards, 14 touchdowns).

He had been a late second-round pick, 65th overall, and his signing bonus as a rookie was $1.025 million. By the time the Patriots traded him to Seattle, the Seahawks had agreed with him on a six-year, $39 million pact.

Troy recalls some conversations he had with Branch before that trade, reminding him that patience would pay off some day. He didn't want to tell Branch what to do, other than support him if he felt that his decision would be in the best interest of his family. While Patriots management and Branch's representatives butted heads, with charges of tampering and a grievance filed against the team, Troy and Deion remained tight.

As for football, Troy looked around the receivers meeting room and figured name tags might be needed. He had significant concern that the team would be able to compete for a championship with its receiving corps that included himself, Reche Caldwell, Chad Jackson, Doug Gabriel, in-season signing Jabar Gaffney, Kelvin Kight, and Bam Childress, among others. Even going back to the Pete Carroll years from 1997 to 1999, he didn't recall such a dearth of talent at the receiver position. Troy missed the camaraderie he had in past years.

On top of all that, he started experiencing significant pain in his knee. He thought he could manage it, but knew there would be a limit and he wouldn't be able to absorb a full workload. He had concern about his own ability to play at a high level.

Caldwell ended up leading the team in receptions with 61, but he had been coming off a torn ACL and it was clear to Troy that he hadn't rehabbed all the way back. He was obviously a step below Deion Branch and David Givens, who had excelled from 2002 to 2005. Caldwell kept things light in the receivers room, but part of the reason he was more of a journeyman was because of inconsistency. You never really knew what you were going to get from him on a daily basis. It could look really good at times. But other times, not so good.

Meanwhile, Gabriel initially pulled his hamstring and Troy noticed pretty quickly that he was the type of player who would need a little more oversight from others on the roster. He wasn't as mentally tough as some of the team's past receivers. If he didn't get it right initially, he seemed to have some trouble getting back on track.

Troy took pride in his leadership role, and did his part in that area, but it was draining at times for him that year. In retrospect, he couldn't believe the team was a play or two away from making it to the Super Bowl, a crushing loss to the Indianapolis Colts in the AFC Championship Game ending the season.

Gaffney ended up breaking through in 2007 more than 2006, but his mental aptitude was clear from the outset. Troy noticed that he picked up a fairly complex offense quicker than most. His presence ended up being important for Troy because it lessened his workload.

Then there was highly touted second-round draft pick Chad Jackson out of Florida. He had the look of a big-time talent, chiseled physique, and a lot of natural gifts. The Patriots were so high on Jackson that they included him in their traditional photo of the No. 1 draft pick, even though he was a second-rounder. So that year, it was running back Laurence Maroney (21st overall) and Jackson (36th overall) getting the star treatment, with owner Robert Kraft jokingly presenting Jackson with a winter jacket because he was coming to town from Florida.

But it just didn't all come together the way the team hoped.

From Troy's viewpoint, Jackson's situation had some similarities to another highly touted receiver from earlier in his career, 2003 second-round draft pick Bethel Johnson. You looked at both players and it was hard not to be impressed with their natural gifts. Johnson was maybe the fastest player in the NFL, but Troy saw a player who wasn't always open to taking instruction. The mental side of the game seemed to be a struggle for him, which is what separated him from other younger receivers who had success, such as Deion Branch and David Givens. Branch and Givens had a humble approach and took a sponge-like approach in learning from everyone else around them.

But that's something you just can't teach a player, even if they have good intentions. Troy never viewed Johnson or Jackson as bad apples. They just had a certain element of cockiness to them, and he could tell how that would wear on quarterback Tom Brady at times. The reason Troy knew that was the case was because it wore on him, too. The spirit of the receivers room was different than it had been in the past; there wasn't the same sense of urgency about the importance of meetings, being on time, and putting in extra time conditioning.

Looking back, Troy views 2006 as one of the toughest years of his career, mainly because of the health of his knee. For maybe the first time he could remember, he had to consider rest as the best approach, rather than working on the field. That didn't come naturally to him, as he took pride in practicing through almost anything, and then staying after practice for extra work. He usually craved the extra repetitions, but in 2006, he backed off, with the mindset that he needed to save that for game day.

So that was a different point in his career, and a different situation for the team, which needed Troy maybe more than either of them figured would be the case at that point in his career. He used to enter games focusing on playing 70 to 80 snaps, but felt at that point he might have been more equipped for 30 to 40.

Despite all the uncertainty, the Patriots opened that season 6–1. Troy started the season-opener and scored the team's first touchdown of the year, a nine-yard reception from Tom Brady in a 19–17 win over the Bills at home.

In Week 2, a rather convincing 24–17 win over the New York Jets on the road, Troy led the team with four catches for 51 yards. The

Patriots opened a 24–0 lead in that game, which marked the first time facing former Patriots defensive coordinator Eric Mangini as Jets coach, before holding off a late charge.

So here was Troy, knowing he wasn't the same player he once was, playing a leading role and trying to fight through a painful knee injury.

The Patriots' lack of weaponry in the passing game and a failure to convert on fourth-and-1 in the first half caught up to them the next week in a 17–7 loss to the Broncos. It was a prime-time game—a matchup of wits between head coaches Bill Belichick and Mike Shanahan—which was followed by wins over the Bengals (38–13), Dolphins (20–10), and Bills (28–6). The game against Miami was one of Troy's best, as he had five catches for 58 yards, which included a 10-yard touchdown reception.

How were the Patriots doing it with such a patchwork receiving corps?

Troy wasn't really sure, but when the team visited the Minnesota Vikings on Monday, October 30, it was a heavily hyped matchup on ESPN between the 6–1 Patriots and the 4–2 Vikings.

In one of the classic Patriots games of that time period, the team rolled to a 31–7 victory. It was how they did it that was impressive. The Vikings had the NFL's top run defense with burly defensive tackles Kevin Williams and Pat Williams, so what did a Patriots team with a rag-tag receiver group do? They spread the field with four and five receivers, favored a pass-first approach, and sliced through Minnesota's defense with relative ease.

Troy had a seven-yard touchdown catch in the fourth quarter as the silence in the since-demolished Metrodome was unforgettable. So too was the message the Patriots had sent to a national audience.

Bill Belichick often reminds his players never to get too high or too low during a season, because there are inevitable ups and downs, and the next two weeks tested them in that area. Losses to the Colts (27–20) and Mangini's Jets (17–14) dropped the Patriots to 6–3 and some of the same questions that had followed the team entering the year were resurfacing.

Did they have enough quality receivers? Were they really Super Bowl contenders or was that unforgettable night in Minnesota the high point?

If one had to pick the Patriots' top rivals of that time period, the Colts and Jets were right near the top of the list, and that was seen by the emotion on the field during those games. When normally mild-mannered Colts wide receiver Marvin Harrison made a sensational diving one-handed catch in the third quarter to produce a four-yard touchdown, he sprung to his feet and spiked the ball with Rob Gronkowski–type force. Harrison almost never reacted that way after a score.

That was also the first game that former Patriots kicker Adam Vinatieri, in his first year as a Colt, returned to Gillette Stadium. A Super Bowl hero, he was still booed.

"They are trying to get loud and make it hard on the opposing team. That totally makes sense," Vinatieri said as the Colts remained undefeated and many declared them the class of the AFC, noting how the tables had turned on the Patriots.

For Troy, the night was memorable from a personal perspective as he broke Stanley Morgan's record for career receptions (534), which would later be broken by Wes Welker.

"I told Troy that if anyone was going to break the record that I was glad it was going to be him," Morgan said. "Troy reminds me so much of myself."

Later that week, the Patriots had a special news conference to honor Troy's accomplishment, with Morgan and owner Robert Kraft.

"We don't recognize individual achievements normally at the Patriots, but Troy would have gotten the game ball had we won after the Colts game," Kraft said at the time. "We tried to create a different scenario that would allow us to celebrate what's been good about the Patriots' history and that would allow us to bring Stanley 'Steamer' back.

"For me, both of these individuals are special. I had looked forward to awarding Troy with a game ball, because he's the only player on the team that has been here for 14 years. I was sitting in the stands the first year he was in the league. He's the prototype Patriot—selfless, offense, defense, special teams. He never did fancy dances, just did what's right both on and off the field.

"Stanley Morgan was the same kind of guy. He was with the team for 13 years. He was one of the half-dozen that I personally rooted for very strongly. He always was very classy and represented what the Patriot brand was always about."

Troy humbly accepted a special football from Kraft that day.

"I want to thank Mr. Kraft and Stanley for the kind words about the way I go out and play the game," he said. "I take a lot of pride in the way I go out there and play, and represent not only myself and my family, but the Kraft family and the organization. I always try to set the right example and show my teammates the right way to out and play the game."

A world-renowned French glassblower named Jean-Claude Novaro made one life-sized statue of Troy and presented it that day. It still sits in the team's lobby at team headquarters, there for visitors to see.

As for the loss to the Jets, that has always been a big rivalry for the Patriots, but it was heightened even more after Mangini, the former Patriots assistant, bolted town to become their head coach after just one season as New England defensive coordinator. One got the sense that Belichick didn't approve of the move, and there was significant attention paid to the postgame handshake between the two. On a rainy night, it was a cold, quick exchange.

"I have a lot of great memories from here," Mangini said after the Jets shattered the Patriots' record of 57 consecutive games without back-to-back losses. "I'd like to add this to it."

"Two losses in a row; I can't remember the last time we did it," Patriots linebacker Tedy Bruschi said. "We've got to get back on the winning road if we want to be AFC champions."

One lighthearted joke around the Patriots was that a loss to the Jets can produce an extreme reaction, and in this case, the club decided to completely change its playing surface. The natural grass, which was a mess on that rainy night against the Jets, was replaced by synthetic grass. The process had to be completed within two weeks, as the team had a road game against the Green Bay Packers before returning to face the Chicago Bears the next week.

The Patriots went 6–1 to finish the season with a 12–4 record.

They rolled over the Packers 35–0, and that game was notable for Troy because he was back on defense and given the challenging assignment of covering receiver Donald Driver. He aced it, with Driver catching just one pass against him, for three yards. It had been a while since Troy had played defense, but his presence was required because starting safeties Eugene Wilson and Rodney Harrison were sidelined, as was top cornerback Asante Samuel.

When Troy ultimately retired two years later, he was presented a picture of himself by Belichick from that game. Belichick told him he thought it epitomized what he's all about—a team-first player who was willing to go back on defense without hesitation and answered the challenge.

The team then returned home to face the Bears in a game that is remembered for, among other things, Tom Brady juking out linebacker Brian Urlacher on an 11-yard run which converted a third-and-9 situation in the fourth quarter. Already, the new playing surface was paying dividends.

Troy himself showed he could still run well the following week, taking an end-around 16 yards in a 28–21 win over the Lions at home. It was a game that turned out to be an escape, the Patriots scoring 15 fourth-quarter points to pull away.

Concerns over the receiving corps resurfaced the following week when the Patriots were shut out 21–0 in a loss at Miami. Tom Brady was held to 78 yards passing as longtime nemesis Jason Taylor harassed him and Brady was visibly frustrated on the field, sometimes yelling at teammates.

But the Patriots exploded the following week to quiet some of that talk, beating the Texans 40–7 before finishing out the year with road wins over the Jaguars (24–21) on Christmas Eve and the Titans (40–23) on New Year's Eve. Troy scored the final touchdown of the regular season, a six-yard grab in the back of the end zone from backup quarterback Vinny Testaverde.

The touchdown was significant for Testaverde, who was 43 at the time, as he set the record for throwing at least one touchdown pass in 20 different seasons.

"I wanted to give it to him. I think he deserves it," coach Bill Belichick said afterward.

The year before, Belichick had given quarterback Doug Flutie the unique opportunity to attempt a drop-kick in the season finale, which was successful. That Troy was on the receiving end of Testaverde's touchdown strike was fitting in a sense because they were the two old guys.

"I'm giddy about the oldest pass reception tandem in the league," defensive lineman Ty Warren cracked in the locker room. "I think it's 100 years of experience between the two of them."

Players celebrated for Testaverde, some coming onto the field, while Belichick held his arms over his head.

Yet as much as the Patriots were excited about that turn of events, they also seethed because the victory came at a cost, with safety Rodney Harrison injuring his right leg on a dangerous block by receiver Bobby Wade that would ultimately end Harrison's season. That was a devastating blow to the Patriots, knowing that they were about to face some of the league's top tight ends and Harrison would have been a big part of their game plans.

It was on to the playoffs, and that's where Troy would make one of the unforgettable plays of his career. Then he would experience one of the most crushing defeats.

* * *

The Patriots' playoff run of 2006 highlighted the essence of Troy Brown's career. Against all odds, and in improbable fashion, he delivered a play for the ages.

The Patriots had beaten Eric Mangini's New York Jets in the wild-card round of the playoffs 37–16, setting up a road trip to take on the top-seeded San Diego Chargers and their dynamic offense, led by running back LaDainian Tomlinson.

It wasn't looking good for Troy and the Patriots midway through the fourth quarter.

The Chargers went ahead 21–13 on a Tomlinson three-yard touchdown run with 8:40 remaining in the game, putting all the pressure on the Patriots, who knew they were likely limited to two possessions the rest of the way to close the gap. Maybe, if they were lucky, there would be a third.

The Tom Brady–led offense advanced the ball into Chargers territory, to the 41-yard line, before facing a critical fourth-and-5 situation. They had to go for it.

That's when Brady looked over the middle and tried to fit the football into a tight window to…who else?…Troy.

When safety Marlon McCree stepped in front of Troy and intercepted it, the stadium erupted. That would be, for all intents and purposes, the dagger that ended the Patriots' season.

"It was fourth-and-5 so if it's incomplete, it's their ball anyway," Brady said of the pass that he probably wouldn't have thrown otherwise. "You're just trying to squeeze it in there."

Yet this is where Troy's never-quit approach rose to the forefront. Instead of submitting to what many figured would be the end result, he did what came natural to him and turned into an aggressive defender. McCree, inexplicably, was trying to run with the ball and Troy jarred the ball out of his grasp. When receiver Reche Caldwell recovered, the Patriots still had a fighting chance.

"It ended up being a big play," Brady said. "He intercepted it, and fortunately he did or else we wouldn't have got the ball back. It definitely wasn't part of the plan."

In so many ways, the play was a microcosm of Troy's career—he simply could never be counted out, even when it seemed like there wasn't a chance. He had been lightly recruited out of high school, landed at Marshall pretty much out of sheer luck (the coach was recruiting someone else and spotted Troy) after a stopover at junior college, and then was an eighth-round draft choice of the Patriots who was out of the NFL one year later wondering if he'd ever play again.

And yet here he was, in Year 14, delivering a play like that. The Patriots had the ball at the Chargers' 32-yard line and five plays later, Brady was connecting with Caldwell, a former Charger, for a four-yard touchdown. Trailing 21–19, the Patriots needed a two-point conversion and they got it on a direct snap to running back Kevin Faulk.

Just like that, the game was tied at 21. If Troy hadn't made that play, the season was probably over.

"Troy Brown…that guy's a terrific football player," Patriots coach Bill Belichick marveled after the game. "He does it all."

The Patriots went on to win 24–21, and McCree was roasted in San Diego. Had he just given himself up by falling to the ground, or even just batted the pass down, the Chargers would have eliminated any unnecessary risk.

"I was trying to make a play, and any time I get the ball I am going to try and score," he explained. "I saw there was a lineman in front of me and I knew if I could make him miss, I was off and running. Before I had a chance to do that, Troy Brown stripped it. He made a great play and I was trying to make a big play. I don't regret it because I would never try and just go down. I want to score."

McCree said he didn't think he could knock down the ball because Brady basically threw it right to him.

"I would do the same thing if I had the same opportunity. This time I would just secure the ball more."

When the Patriots' defense held the Chargers to a three-and-out on the ensuing drive, they took over at their own 15-yard line and drove to the San Diego 12 to set up the game-winning field goal. A 49-yard-long bomb from Brady to Caldwell was the key play to set it up.

It was a most improbable win—the Patriots scoring 11 unanswered points in the fourth quarter to steal the game. Players celebrated on the field after the game, some mocking the celebratory dance of San Diego pass-rusher Shawne Merriman, which drew the ire of running back LaDanian Tomlinson.

"They showed no class," Tomlinson said. "Maybe it comes from the head coach."

Meanwhile, Patriots linebacker Tedy Bruschi described the result as "against all odds." That Troy was right in the middle of it was hardly surprising.

"If I don't get the ball stripped away from me at the end of the game, I think we win," the Chargers' McCree said.

They didn't, which set the Patriots up with a road trip to Indianapolis where they would face Peyton Manning and the Indianapolis Colts in the AFC Championship Game.

As much elation as Troy had from making such a critical play against the Chargers, he would experience the opposite end of the spectrum in a crushing 38–34 defeat that day. New England led 21–3 early in the second quarter, weathered a ferocious comeback, and ultimately held a 34–31 lead with 3:49 remaining before Manning led the Colts down the field for the game-winning touchdown.

Troy would later have a feeling of great pride when discussing the accomplishments of the 2006 Patriots team. Many were surprised at how far the Patriots had advanced, and how productive they were on offense, considering that might have been the least talented receiving corps Troy had ever been a part of in professional football. Meanwhile, he didn't view that year's defense as one of the better units either. It was solid, no doubt, but without the likes of cornerback Ty Law and others, it just wasn't the same, as the results of the AFC Championship Game showed.

Privately, Troy and his teammates viewed the game against the

Colts as the Super Bowl because they felt confident that whichever team came out of the NFC (it ended up being the Bears) wasn't going to be as much of a threat. Troy felt like the Patriots could match up against the physicality of either NFC team, which would have been a contrast to the more finesse approach of the Colts.

Thus, Troy still thinks about the AFC Championship Game against the Colts. It's one of those games that weighs on his mind as he wonders what it would have been like to earn a fourth Super Bowl championship. If one or two plays unfolded differently, maybe it's a different story.

One play, in particular, still nags at Troy, as it helped keep the game close at a time when the Patriots were in position to increase their 21–3 lead. There was 4:32 remaining in the second quarter, and facing a third-and-6, the Patriots converted when Tom Brady found tight end Benjamin Watson for a nine-yard gain that advanced the ball to the Colts' 19-yard line.

At that point, the worst-case scenario for the Patriots seemed to be a field goal that would increase the lead to 24–3, but it turned out there was something even worse than that—a penalty on Troy for offensive pass interference that negated the play. Instead of first-and-10 at the 19, it was third-and-16 from the Colts' 38.

Troy can still see the play in slow motion, running through this head almost a decade later. From his recollection, it was the worst offensive pass interference penalty ever called against him.

He felt so strongly about it because it was the defender who had initiated contact, not him. Troy simply bounced off him, creating traffic that allowed Watson to be uncovered in the flat to make the play. Troy suspected the defender was assigned to cover Watson and when he knew he was in trouble, he sold the penalty hard and the official took the bait.

The Patriots had run the same play often, with Troy catching hundreds of footballs, and what irritated him even more about the penalty was that it seemed reactionary. From Troy's view, only after the referee saw how open Watson was in the flat did he throw the flag.

"He ran into me, jammed me, and I'm the one getting called for offensive pass interference?" Troy thought to himself on the sideline.

Of all the plays in Troy's career, that's one that still bothers him. He wasn't setting an illegal pick, as the referee deemed. In later years, he would later compare the Patriots' good fortune with the "Tuck Rule" to that penalty as things on the opposite end of the spectrum when it came to a referee's decision having a positive or negative impact on the game. Maybe, at that moment, he empathized with the 2001 Raiders a bit.

The game started to shift after the play. A false start pushed the Patriots back even farther and they ended up punting after Tom Brady was sacked to knock them out of field goal range. When the Colts went on a long drive that ended with a field goal, slicing the Patriots' lead to 21–6, it was easy to see that the second half was setting up as a classic.

The Colts, much like the St. Louis Rams and "the Greatest Show on Turf" of 2001, could score points quickly. A 15-point lead could disappear in a hurry.

That's exactly what happened to the Patriots, as the Colts went on a 14-play, 76-yard touchdown drive to open the third quarter. It covered 6:47 and the New England defense, which badly missed the injured Rodney Harrison, was on its heels.

Then came a three-and-out on offense, another Colts touchdown, and with four minutes remaining in the third quarter, the game was tied at 21.

From that point, it was a back-and-forth thriller. The teams traded touchdowns—28-all—then punts, then field goals—31-all.

When the Patriots went ahead 34–31 with 3:51 remaining, and then forced a punt with a defensive stop, they had their best chance to win. Getting the ball back with 3:22 remaining, the goal, naturally, was to not let Manning and the Colts have the ball back with too much time left on the clock.

Much like the offensive pass interference penalty that still irks him today, Troy has had trouble letting go of how that drive began. Before the Patriots could even snap the ball on first-and-10, they were penalized for having 12 men in the huddle.

Troy was in the huddle at the time, saw the confusion, and tried to save the situation by stepping out and removing himself. No luck. Referee Bill Carollo flagged the Patriots, setting up first-and-15 from the Patriots' 35-yard line.

That still isn't a bad situation when it comes to field position, but staying on schedule against a team like the Colts is always the goal. When they get you into obvious passing situations, that's when they are at their best with their ferocious edge pressure.

The Patriots executed two short passes—a seven-yarder to Reche Caldwell and a four-yarder to Benjamin Watson, the latter of which forced the Colts to burn their second timeout to stop the clock. That set up third-and-4 and Troy, just like he was the week before against the Chargers, was the focal point of a key play.

Only this time, the end result was crushing.

Troy remembers being in the huddle and hearing Brady call a play before instructing him to "break it outside." Before the snap, Troy motioned toward the line of scrimmage, but the corner didn't follow him, which led Troy to second-guess the idea of breaking his route outside because he'd be going directly into the area where the cornerback was playing.

When the ball was snapped, Troy recognized the Colts' scheme as what is sometimes referred to as "robber coverage," which happens with a safety coming down (in this case it was Bob Sanders) toward the line of scrimmage. As this was unfolding, Troy had it in the back of his mind that Brady had told him to break outside, but based on the corner staying so wide, he didn't think it was possible.

So Troy altered the route, pushing out wide and then hooking back, hoping that they'd be on the same page. They weren't, as Brady's pass was almost intercepted by Sanders, the safety, who nearly had a pick-6. So the Patriots had to punt it away and hope the defense could come up with one more stop.

Meanwhile, Brady and Troy had a spirited conversation as they walked off the field that reflected the intensity of the moment.

"I told you to break outside!" Brady shouted in Troy's direction.

"It wasn't possible," Troy yelled back, noting the presence of the cornerback who stayed wide.

Brady's fire is well documented and naturally Bill Belichick was curious about what had happened, so he joined the discussion. That's when Troy told him he felt like he didn't have much of a choice on the play because of the positioning of the cornerback.

"Just didn't feel like I could go there," Troy told him.

The Colts went on to score a touchdown, driving 80 yards in just 1:02. The Patriots had a last-gasp attempt but Brady's pass over the middle was intercepted and the team was dealt a bitter defeat. In those types of situations, players often reflect on the one or two plays that could have possibly turned the outcome. For Troy, it was the offensive pass interference penalty in the second quarter and the third-and-4 incompletion when Brady wanted him to break outside.

In the heat of the moment, players will react in a way that they might otherwise not and it wasn't until they were on the plane home that Brady and Troy furthered their discussion about the disappointing third-down play. Troy left the conversation feeling as if Brady understood the decision he made based on the coverage.

Still, Troy couldn't help but feel he had let the team down. Just one week earlier, he had been the hero by jarring the ball free from Marlon McCree, and now this.

So it goes sometimes in the game of football. It would be a long off-season for him to digest it all.

Thirteen

A BEHIND-THE-SCENES VIEW OF A NEAR-PERFECT SEASON

The Patriots have a hard-driving culture, and Moss' reputation sparked questions as to how things would work out.

CHAPTER THIRTEEN

A Behind-the-Scenes View of a Near-Perfect Season

As time passed, Troy gained more and more appreciation for what the 2006 team had accomplished. What they lacked in talent they made up for in toughness—both physically and mentally. Those are the main ingredients of some of Bill Belichick's most successful teams.

Sometimes you go further with less talent, and that's the way he viewed that year.

By 2007, the Patriots' talent at receiver improved dramatically. It was almost as if Bill Belichick made it a point to load up after what unfolded in '06 when Reche Caldwell was the leading receiver, so he traded for Wes Welker and Randy Moss, and also signed Donte Stallworth.

As for Troy, he was a free agent and it was unclear how things would unfold. He'd undergone knee surgery after the season and he was questioning whether to play a 15th season or retire.

With the Patriots in a holding pattern, leaving the ball in Troy's court, the rival Jets and their second-year head coach Eric Mangini moved the process along by inviting Troy to town for a free-agent visit. Troy tried to envision himself playing for the Jets—the green and white colors of their uniforms matched those of his college days at Marshall—which would have been a stunning turn of events.

In truth, the Patriots were probably hoping he'd retire. But when the Jets showed a willingness to offer him a contract, and Troy decided he wanted to play another season, the situation hung in the balance for a short while. Creating further uncertainty was that it was unclear how Troy would recover from his knee surgery, and how the Patriots had dramatically revamped their receiver corps.

The knee was an issue and Troy remembers talking with linebacker Tedy Bruschi about it, as Bruschi had a similar surgery that involved the tendon. What stood out to Troy was that Bruschi said it took him about a full year to feel like himself again. At this point, Troy was 36 years old, which is basically senior citizen status in the NFL.

Troy ended up re-signing with the Patriots, with owner Robert Kraft getting involved because he wanted to ensure that Troy finished his career with the franchise. There was an understanding behind the scenes that this would be Troy's final season. Troy felt his heart was in New England, and looking back, the organization took care of him that final year by signing him to a contract despite his knee issue and restocked receiving corps.

Troy opened that year on the reserve/physically unable to perform list and ended up playing in just one game all season. Had one of the top-line receivers been injured, maybe it would have been different, but Troy couldn't really argue with it because Wes Welker was having great success in Troy's former role as the primary slot receiver.

Troy had heard Bill Belichick speak highly of Welker when the team was preparing to play Welker's former team, the Dolphins.

When the Patriots acquired him for a second-round pick, Troy knew it was a steal, despite what many in the media said about the Patriots overpaying for a "slot" receiver. In the Patriots' offense, the slot receiver might as well be what many call a "No. 1 receiver" anyway.

Then there was Randy Moss. Troy had the obvious connection with him, as both were Marshall alums, but he remembers that there were still a lot of questions in the locker room among players as to how he would fit in. The Patriots have a hard-driving culture, and Moss' reputation sparked questions as to how things would work out. Troy himself wondered if it all might backfire, curious if the team was now headed in an unfamiliar direction.

At the same time, Troy could tell how excited Tom Brady was to work with Moss, especially after the rag-tag group he was throwing to in 2006. As it turned out, the results were explosive, with Brady setting the NFL record for touchdown passes in a season and Moss setting the NFL record for touchdown receptions in a season.

What Troy saw from Moss behind the scenes impressed him, as he was fully committed to the team. At the same time, he was loud, had fun, and worked hard to fit into the well-established locker-room culture. He was a regular film watcher, studied hard, often had new ideas for coaches to consider, and most importantly hit it off with Brady.

Sometimes a personality like that can be diva-like and want to dominate the meeting room, but Troy didn't see it that way with Moss. By the end of the year, Troy summed up Moss in two words: "great teammate."

That taught him a lesson of sorts, because he had heard all the stories about Moss from Oakland and Minnesota. Anyone could have judged him at the time, but by giving him a chance, Troy got to create his own impression and it was a favorable one.

He knew it was going to be a special year as early as training camp. After finishing his rehabilitation, Troy would walk up to the two fields behind Gillette Stadium and watch practice, and like others his jaw dropped at times when seeing some of the things Moss could do. It was clear there was an immediate connection between Brady and Moss. No matter what defense was called, or where Brady decided to throw to Moss, it just worked. Sometimes it seemed so simple—just drop back and chuck it.

Troy had worked out with Moss at Marshall, so he had seen some of the "freak-like" things he could do, but to see it consistently every day, it almost felt like a privilege. What stood out to him was how Moss would run "go" and post routes and it looked so effortless. He was picking up speed and before you knew it, he was racing past you, even though it hardly looked like he was running fast. Specifically, Moss had the ability to accelerate when the ball was in the air and he was always relaxed and under control throughout the route. As long as the quarterback put the ball in the neighborhood, there was a chance to make the play because of his leaping ability.

Troy himself played in one game that season, a 28–7 victory over the Miami Dolphins on December 23. He spent most of the year on the reserve/physically unable to perform list before being activated late in the year. When he made his first play of the season, a 10-yard punt return in the first quarter, it marked his 192nd career game, which at the time was the fourth most in team history. His 15 straight years with the team tied Jason Elam (Broncos) and Michael Strahan (Giants) for the second longest tenure with the same team among current players at the time.

As one would expect, Troy was a bit rusty that day, muffing a punt in the second quarter that the Dolphins recovered. But the Patriots were never in jeopardy of losing the game and Troy pretty much knew that would probably be his last game as a Patriot at Gillette Stadium. His final play was a 28-yard punt return.

That made Troy's final season in the NFL unlike any other. In one respect, it hurt to not be able to contribute. But to have a behind-the-scenes front-row seat for one of the all-time great seasons in NFL history was meaningful in its own way, and also included the Spygate controversy, in which the Patriots were penalized for filming opponents' signals from a prohibited location.

The story broke after the Patriots' 38–14 season-opening victory over the Jets, and spread like wildfire. The ironic part about it from Troy's perspective was that he had no idea what it was all about. He said he's never seen a tape of another team that wasn't the standard game film, and had no idea of any illegal activity taking place. So when people would ask him about it, he'd simply answer, "I have no idea what it's all about."

At the same time, Troy and his teammates could feel tension in the building that week, and many in the media began questioning the Patriots. Troy remembers how Bill Belichick addressed the team, saying something along the lines of, "This situation has nothing to do with you; I'll take care of it, so leave it to me and just focus on doing your job." Owner Robert Kraft was present for that team meeting.

To Troy, that was the end of it. At times it seemed like that was the only thing the media wanted to talk about and it raised the ire of some players. But the way Troy remembers it, that wasn't a hot topic of discussion when it came to locker-room banter that year. While some said players were motivated by everything that had unfolded, Troy didn't see it that way.

The way he viewed that 2007 team, it was more of a business-like approach among players. They knew they had the chance to do something special, perhaps that had never been done before, and most players adopted a laser-like focus throughout.

The Patriots finished the regular season with a 16–0 record and they made it look like a video game at times, putting up eye-popping point totals. Through the first seven games of the year, they were averaging 41.3 points per contest. Some grilled them for running up the score.

As the calendar turned to late November, however, Troy noticed that teams started to figure some things out in terms of slowing the Patriots' high-flying offense down a bit. The gap was closing. A 27–24 win at Baltimore on December 3 would have been a loss if then-Ravens defensive coordinator Rex Ryan hadn't called an ill-advised timeout late in the game.

But the Patriots gutted it out, and after beating the Jacksonville Jaguars and San Diego Chargers in the playoffs, they went to Super Bowl XLII in Glendale, Arizona, with an 18–0 record and needing only to top the New York Giants to become the first wire-to-wire undefeated team since the '72 Dolphins.

While many were talking about the Patriots' potential perfect season, Troy's view behind the scenes was different. He had legitimate concern for the team entering the game because practices were less than perfect.

Over his 15 years in professional football, he had never been part of a team that practiced as poorly as the Patriots did leading up to the most important game of their careers, which led to them being kicked off the field by Bill Belichick at one point. There was maybe one other time, under Bill Parcells in the mid 1990s, that Troy remembers coaches reacting with the same level of disgust. Back then, Parcells simply walked off the field and decided he wasn't coaching the team that day because players were making so many miscues.

It was puzzling to Troy leading into the Super Bowl, because the Patriots had shown they were capable of so much that season, but in practice a simple completion seemed elusive. The concepts they had mastered throughout the year, such as receivers running combination routes, were botched. Meanwhile, the defense was struggling with its adjustments and to make the right calls.

Troy felt the team's first two practices upon arriving in Arizona were as bad as he's been a part of at any level, and by the end of the week, things had picked up slightly but it was still an uneasy feeling. Legendary running back Jim Brown was a guest of Bill Belichick for one practice, with Troy remembering that he told players they had a chance to do something special.

Troy knew he'd be inactive for the Super Bowl—everyone was healthy, he had only appeared in one game all season and was mostly doing scout-team work—but he still wanted the victory as bad as any other. He privately wondered if too many players were distracted, and if the focus was in the right place—on the game and not the overall Super Bowl atmosphere, such as their plans each night. Confidence is good, but he sensed almost a little cockiness, which didn't feel right to him.

As one of the team's leaders by example, he was disappointed in what he was seeing, but also in a spot that was hard for him to make a difference. When you're not playing, it's hard to stand on the front lines and call for a correction of sorts.

One Super Bowl "tradition" among Patriots players had been to take pictures with position coaches, in addition to group pictures with players' families who were present. But when the effort was made to get everyone together the day before the Super Bowl, some players had simply taken off and weren't available. Troy tried to get them back, with no success.

So when he looks back on his personal photographs from that Super Bowl, the absence of a group photo stands out to him. It sounds minor, but because teams change on a year-to-year basis and Troy figured this was almost certainly the last year of his career, that left a void of sorts. Some might call it bad karma.

As for not playing in the Super Bowl, it didn't compare to the sting Troy had felt in the 1996 season when he didn't play because of injury. That one was much worse for him.

Yet it didn't make what unfolded that night any easier for him to accept. As a competitor, he couldn't help but think to himself, "Maybe if I was out there, I could have helped." Of course, had Giants receiver David Tyree not caught a football on his helmet, or cornerback Asante Samuel came down with an interception, the whole storyline would have been different. It was Tyree's fluke play that most contributed to the Patriots losing a 17–14 heartbreaker.

In the end, Troy had to give the Giants credit for a plan that gave the Patriots a lot of trouble. As much as the Patriots had practiced poorly, reinforcing the idea that a team will play like it practices, that shouldn't diminish the effort put forth by the Giants. Troy compared their effort and performance to the Patriots' in Super Bowl XXXVI against the St. Louis Rams. Much like the Patriots that year, the Giants were determined to make it a physical game, on the perimeter and up front on their defensive line, where they essentially sold out against the pass and decided that if the Patriots wanted to run, they'd deal with the consequences.

Another similarity between the Patriots-Rams and Patriots-Giants Super Bowls was that the teams had met during the regular season, which gave the underdog in each game some confidence.

It was a result that shocked the world, although based on what he had seen in the practices leading up to the game, Troy wasn't overly surprised. With so much at stake, the Patriots weren't at their best.

And now, with his football career coming to a close, Troy had to consider where his life would take him next.

Fourteen

IT'S HARD TO WALK
AWAY FROM THE
GAME YOU LOVE

He was practicing one day in training camp, looked around, and said "I don't fit in here anymore."

CHAPTER FOURTEEN

It's Hard to Walk Away From the Game You Love

It's hard to walk away from a game you love so much and has been part of your life since the second grade. Troy started playing when he was seven years old, and here he was at age 37, and he would have loved to hang on for another year. The game, in so many ways, had been good to him.

The Jets had offered him a contract for 2008, but Troy decided at that point it was the Patriots or retirement. And there were days he wondered if he might have been able to sneak out a 16th season with the organization. Sometimes he'd wonder how things might have been different if the Patriots were still playing on natural grass, which was a better surface for his sometimes troublesome knee.

At that point, Troy would envision what it might be like playing another season. That's why he kept working out throughout the off-season, kept close tabs on any free-agent signings and what it might mean for him. There was a thought in the back of his mind that if his knee suddenly felt better, maybe he'd give it a shot.

At the same time, he knew when he came back in 2007, it would probably be his last season. And the way that one turned out—playing

215

just one game—he knew it was probably time to say goodbye.

Still, there were questions lingering that he really didn't want to answer. What am I going to do if this is really it? What can possibly match what the game has meant to me?

It's emotional and the way Troy describes it, it just hit him one day unexpectedly. He remembers hearing his good friend David Patten say the same thing happened to him; he was practicing one day in training camp, looked around, and said, "I don't fit in here anymore."

That's what happened to Troy as he was spending the day at his alma mater, Marshall, where he was in the middle of a workout running sprints and routes when he looked up and thought to himself, "Man, I'm tired. I'm sore. What am I doing here?"

Troy stopped his workout, picked up his belongings, went home, and called the Patriots. His message: "I'm ready to go. I'm ready to retire."

For some players, that decision comes quickly and it's not their choice. For Troy, it was more gradual and the Patriots gave him the respect and room to get there on his own. He had earned that and he knew the day was close; he just wasn't sure when.

His final two seasons, 2006 and 2007, were a struggle on and off the field. In a young man's game, Troy was the old guy whose level of participation wasn't as high as it used to be. In the earlier years of his career, he had usually recovered from the previous game by Wednesday, which often marked the first day of practice for the next contest. But in '06 and '07, Wednesdays were especially tough for Troy. He had heavy weightlifting on Monday, an off day Tuesday, and then it was back to the grind Wednesday, but he struggled with it. It's sort of like putting your foot down on the accelerator of the car and realizing that the car isn't going as fast as you want it.

The struggle was so bad, in fact, that receivers coach Brian Daboll made sure Troy got that day off. Troy tried different things to change the direction things were headed—altering his diet, for example—but there's no escaping Father Time.

Then when Troy went back to Marshall to work out, it wasn't like the old days when he knew he'd see quarterbacks Byron Leftwich and Chad Pennington there, and they'd work out together. As he got older, it was harder to find players to connect with, so he often worked out alone. It was depressing at times.

In the Patriots' locker room, the music reminded Troy that he was the senior citizen in the room. He liked to listen to 1980s rap, R&B, and soul music, and many of the younger players would rib him. Troy remembers thinking to himself, "I wonder if Patriots and Pro Football Hall of Famer Andre Tippett thought the same thing in his final years?" It all contributed to the same type of feeling he said David Patten told him about in his own situation, how he didn't feel like he fit any more. It wasn't that Troy didn't feel part of the team, it's just that bridging the gap with the younger generation was a challenge. While many of them would go out together, Troy was more inclined to be in his bed early because if he wasn't, it would be even more of a struggle the next day.

So he was ready to take this next step and when he arrived in town for his retirement news conference on September 25, 2008, Troy was asked by Bill Belichick to address the team.

His message was how special being part of the Patriots was to him, and how grateful he was for all of them. He'd now be playing the game through them. Troy looked at players like running back Kevin Faulk and told him it was an honor to have been his teammate. Ditto for the likes of Tedy Bruschi and Rodney Harrison, and he came close to crying. It was as emotional as Troy had been, the retirement hitting home. There were a lot of memories in that meeting room.

After Troy delivered those words, it was time for his official retirement news conference and owner Robert Kraft put together a first-class ceremony that day.

"Welcome everyone. I want to welcome Troy [Brown] back to his home here at Gillette Stadium," Kraft began. "I was thinking back that it was 14 years ago when we bought the team. Since that time we have had three head coaches, dozens of assistant coaches, and 820 players. There is only one player that has been a constant through that whole period, who was actually here before my family got here right through the end of last season. How lucky for us that Troy Brown, to me, is the consummate Patriot.

"What he did on the field and the way he conducted himself off the field, the fact that he always put team first, that he stayed with the Patriots his whole career, he could have gone some other places and got more money and he chose to stay here. I think it's a great lesson for the young players on our team today who are worried about making the team.

"Troy was actually drafted in the eighth round in 1993. So today he would be an undrafted free agent because there is no eighth round. Then, he started as a punt returner and a kick returner. In '97, he started as a wide receiver and then his contributions mounted and mounted. In the '01 season he broke the team record for receptions and had over 100 receptions but what sticks out most to me was what he did on special teams that year, especially in the Pittsburgh game, the [AFC] championship game. He returned a Josh Miller punt for 55 yards right up the middle and then he blocked a field goal kick that he 'lateraled' to a teammate, so he was responsible for 14 points alone on special teams that year. Then of course in '04 he played the nickel back role when we needed him as well as being an outstanding wide receiver. As I think back to all the wonderful years with him, I am also so proud about what he represents as a human being. He is a wonderful father and I am happy to see his two sons [Sir'mon and SaanJay] here and his beautiful wife [Kimberly]. He is a responsible family man. He is someone who whatever he has done off the field, whenever someone talks about Troy Brown they talk about what a good human being he is and what [a] good name he has."

Kraft then turned things over to head coach Bill Belichick.

"It has truly been an honor and a privilege to coach Troy, primarily since I came back in 2000, but even my association with him in '96 when I was here as the secondary coach. I think Troy, as I have talked about with our players, is the consummate professional. A great story, a guy that didn't have a college scholarship and got the last scholarship at Marshall. As Robert mentioned, [he was] drafted in the eighth round and we now have seven-round drafts. I think that sums that up," Belichick said.

"When I was in Cleveland and I talked to Coach [Bill] Parcells, I think it was the year after, it was probably in '94, he said, 'We've got this kid from Marshall, a return guy, I don't know if he is any good or not, but there are some things I kind of like about him.' Then, when I got here in '96 and worked against Troy coaching the secondary. There were some good receivers on that team, but in all honesty, we had as much trouble covering Troy as we had covering any of those other guys.

"When [offensive coordinator] Charlie [Weis] and I were at the Jets and then I ultimately came back in 2000, I remember Charlie and I had several conversations about this guy who's really a good football player and he hasn't had the opportunity; what we really thought he could do as a slot receiver and as a deceptive big-play receiver, his versatility in the kicking game.

"Troy has gone on to have a tremendous career here with the most catches in franchise history and 120 catches in that '01 season, including the playoffs. I think back fondly on some of the great moments Troy had here, offensively. The pass from David Patten in the Indianapolis game was a huge play for us in a big game. The Super Bowl, the pass across the middle where he got out of bounds and we had no timeouts to stop the clock and set up the game-winning field goal.

"Against Carolina in '03, in the Super Bowl, he had three catches on that last touchdown, game-winning drive; which without that first-and-20, I don't know where that drive ends up. He made a great catch over the middle from Tom [Brady]. The Snow Game, everybody talks about Adam's [Vinatieri] kick and it was a hell of a kick. But without Troy's punt return to set that up that put us in field position to at least get into field goal range, I don't know if there ever is a kick.

"We got into the '04 season and we had some injuries in the secondary. We used Troy at the inside position in our sub defense in a position we call the 'Star.' I remember the first game we played; it was in St. Louis. That game was against, obviously, still a great offensive football team and he had a big day there, defensively, and broke up some passes. He really stepped in and played a big role in that game and, also, caught probably the easiest touchdown of his career—the sleeper pass down there from Vinatieri on the 4-yard line on the fake field goal. Then, of course, he had the interception against [Drew] Bledsoe and the interception in the Cincinnati game against Carson Palmer to kind of seal that win.

"He just made some plays for us on the defensive side of the ball, but the game that really stands out, to me, is the Green Bay game. We went up there in '06. Eugene Wilson was out. Rodney Harrison was out and Asante [Samuel] was out. We said, 'Well, we're going to put Troy on Donald Driver.' I remember some looks in there from the defensive coaches, and even the players. [Driver] had 93 catches and 1,300 yards. Driver was the leading receiver in the NFC. Troy held him to one catch for three yards. The only one that he caught, Troy wasn't involved in that one, but he had one catch for three yards on him against Donald Driver.

"In the hallways, and the meeting rooms and so forth, we have pictures up from different games and different players. [Holding up a picture of Brown] To me, that picture—and I want to give Troy these pictures from the team—that picture epitomizes Troy Brown. Up against the best receiver in the NFC, in a game that three of our key defensive backs were out, he steps up and does a great job on him.

"I remember the Miami game, in Miami, when we couldn't win in Miami in the early part of the year. I don't know how long...I don't think we'd ever done it. We'd never won in Miami and it didn't look like we were going to that day either. It was 13–13 with six minutes to go in overtime. We couldn't move the ball. It was a tough day. Charlie [Weis] called a 130 Gap Slant. Tom [Brady] looks to the weak side and doesn't have it. Troy runs the post, gets in there behind the safeties and probably gives us one of his biggest catches—it was his longest, 82 yards—to beat Miami when nobody thought we could do that. Nobody thought Troy could go deep. Nobody thought he could make the big plays. But all he did was make plays. He just kept making them.

"I think back to the '01 season when Troy had all of those punt returns: the Oakland game; the Pittsburgh game, for a touchdown; and the Cleveland game. We were sitting there at 7–5. It's a tough game, 10–10, back-and-forth, neither team could really get much of an advantage, and Troy takes that one back, right up the middle. That's the touchdown against Cleveland. Richard Seymour made the block on [Chris] Gardocki. I don't think Troy needed it, but that was a nice block on that touchdown.

"Troy, we have so many great memories of you and all you have done for this organization, this football team and me, personally. I will be forever grateful and indebted to you. It truly has been an honor, truly an honor to coach you as a professional football player. On behalf of our football team and myself, I want to give you these three pictures, three of our greatest memories of you, along with many. Congratulations."

And with that Troy took center stage to close this chapter in his playing career.

"Thank you for coming out today to help cover this event. I am going to try to get through this without crying today. I wanted to come here and share with you the announcement of my retirement from the National Football League and most importantly from the Patriots. I will always be a Patriot, just not in uniform," he began.

"I have been invited by Bill [Belichick]; I am always welcome in the building so I am going to take advantage of that invitation. I wanted to come and share my thoughts with you guys, before you see me pop up somewhere just sitting on TV talking about what am I doing with my life right now. Thank you for coming out and being a part of this. I want to thank Mr. Kraft and his family for allowing me to not just be a part of their football team but a part of their family. He came in after my first season and the team was threatening to move to St. Louis; he came in and saved the day. He kept the team here in New England. If you just look outside of this building now, you can see what a transformation he has made from Foxboro Stadium, not just on this football team but in this community and in the New England area. He has done a tremendous job with building not only his own brand but the NFL brand and bringing them a consistent win year after year. I want to say thank you again to you and your family for keeping me around here for so many years. I know you fought a few years to keep me around. You [Robert Kraft] and Bill [Belichick] were probably going back and forth saying, 'Is he too old yet?' He wanted to keep me around, so I want to thank you. I do appreciate it.

"I want to thank Bill for just believing in me. It was hard for me in the first few years of my career to find that one coach that thought I had what it takes to be a starting receiver in this league. Bill, as you already know, has an eye for talent and eye for identifying the ability to get things done the way he wants them done. Not only the ability but [also] the smarts to play the game the way he likes to play it. He came in here and taught me the right way to play this football game. I tell you, it has been nothing but beneficial to me not only in football but in other areas of my life too. I want to say thank you to him for giving me the opportunity to be something that everyone said I wasn't going to be and that was to be a starting receiver in this league. Not only that but you made me quite a defensive back also. So thank you coach, I do appreciate it.

"Like you said, we share so many memories. I am sure down the line we will share many more—many more stories about the games that we had together and the games that you have coming up in the future too. We will talk a lot of football. That is the one thing I enjoy doing, is talking about the sport that I loved so much and that I played for 30 years. That's why it's hard for guys like myself to let the game go. It has been a part of my life since the second grade—for 30 years. At some point, you reach that point that your mind keeps telling you…I remember watching the games this weekend and it was a tough catch, the guy may not make it and you just tell yourself, 'I can make that play.' But, you get up go outside for a run and, 'Oh, my knee doesn't feel quite right.' You start telling yourself, 'I don't know if I can make that catch or not.' You can't outrun time; no matter how much you try you can't do it. God knows I would love to go out there and try today and practice today but we all know there comes a time where you just have to say, 'I can't keep up anymore.' I would love to play this game the way I played when I was 25, but I just can't keep up the way I used to. I just want to thank you for being here to be a part of this.

"Before I close this up, I want to say thank you to my family for being here. I know it has been tough. It's been hard over the years, being away and being gone, working all the time. Coming home after a bad practice being cussed out by Bill, some of those days are rough. I think I was able to share with you, my wife Kim, my boys Sir'mon and SaanJay, all the success that these guys helped bring about in my life, capturing the ultimate goal, which is to win championships. Not only one, but having an opportunity to play in five of those championship games, bringing home three beautiful rings and capturing that ultimate goal that we all work for and that's to be called a champion. To share that with my boys, to have them on the field with me before the game, letting them be a part of that and what the atmosphere is all about—the confetti falling on their heads. My youngest was three years old the second time we went and he still remembers that confetti falling on his head—that's what this game is all about. It has created some beautiful memories not just for me but [also] for all of you, my family, my friends, and everybody.

"It is hard sometimes to just let it go but I know at the end of the day I played this game the way it was supposed to be played and that's doing whatever it takes to win the game. Not just catching the football, not just lifting weights but a combination of so many different things that goes into building champions. The hard work, dedication, studying, like Bill always said he wanted a smart, tough football team. That's what I always tried to give, whatever my coach asked me to do. That's what I always tried to pass [on] to all the younger guys that came in to show them how I worked in the weight room. Show them how I studied films. Show them how I worked on the field. I think I set a standard here for New England football over the years and it gives me a lot of pleasure and makes me feel good that I know I helped build what's happening here today.

"I didn't do it by myself; a lot of people helped me behind the scenes, on the scene, and at home. It took a lot to build a legacy that is built around here today and the expectations that are formed around here to build champions. I know Bill, I know Mr. Kraft—they won't accept anything less than your best. When you go out and give your best even when your back is up against the wall, people may be doubting you, the kind of situation we are in right now with people doubting the Patriots, doubting us if we can get it done or not. I have been in that situation many times and it helps a lot when you have the confidence of someone that has accomplished as much as these two guys have—to be on your side, to have your back, have your family behind you, and have your friends behind you, to go out there and get your job done. I believe with all my heart when everyone is on the same page and everyone is working together, nothing but great things can happen. That's how I sum up my career. I put the work in. I earned it. I came to work and I did my job. I didn't know where it was going to be everyday but when I got it, I did my job and I did it the best that I could.

"In closing, I want to thank everybody for being a part of my career and helping it to become what it's become. The media, you helped build what's here now. I don't know how to close this thing out. It's hard. It's tough. I would give anything in the world to put those pads on again and do it. I probably had the opportunity to do it but it just wasn't the right color. I didn't think I looked good in green and white again. In closing this thing out, it will be the only colors you ever see on my back as a football player and that's the red, white, and blue of the New England Patriots. I am proud to say that and thank you for all the great memories you all provided. I am almost there before I cry. It's been a wonderful ride. I can't think of anything better in life to do than to enjoy a sunny afternoon playing football. I enjoy those sunny afternoons watching football and still saying in my head, 'I can make that play.'"

As his family and friends watched from the front rows of the news conference, Troy then answered questions from media members.

His personal highlights: "I would say that 82-yard pass in the Miami game [in overtime in 2003]. We hadn't won a game down there in the month of September. To go down there and win that game the way we won it because no one was expecting me to run a deep pattern because I hadn't done that too often before. To end the game the way we did down there, to get that monkey off our back of not winning in September, I thought that was probably one of the biggest plays I can remember."

On whether he ever doubted he could make it in the NFL: "I don't think I ever doubted. When I did get cut my second year, I think I was out about seven or eight weeks, I believe. There was a little bit of doubt that crept into my mind that I wouldn't get a chance to show that I could play in the league. But I don't think I doubted that I could because I had been here and I saw what I was up against. I knew if I had the opportunities that some of those guys had to make the team; I knew that I could show them that I belonged in the NFL. I never doubted myself as far as my ability to play."

The next step in his life: "I plan on suiting up today and going to practice with the guys, but I doubt that will happen. That's my biggest wish. I think you will probably see me around, doing some media stuff, covering a few of the games. You will still see me out doing charity work in the community. That's always been close and dear to my heart, being able to get out, and help people, and put some smiles on some faces. You will still see me around doing quite a few things. I have different business ventures here in town. I will be around. I will be here. This is my second home. I have two homes: West Virginia and Massachusetts."

On any desire to stay involved in the NFL: "At this time, I don't see it happening right now. It sounds like I have some pretty good guys on my side if I wanted to coach. I think right now, whatever I wanted to do, they would help me do it. But, I just don't see it. My boys are not old enough to ride their bikes over to see me at work and that would be the case if I got into coaching. I don't think that's going to happen right now. Maybe when they get a little older I would think about it."

On turning down an offer from the Saints prior to the 2005 season: "It was pretty tempting. It was more money. I think my role here was starting to diminish or had diminished. It's something that my boys, they didn't want to go to New Orleans. They had a lot to do with that decision that year. They didn't want to see me in another uniform besides playing for the Patriots and that was a huge influence for me. I am glad I made that decision. That was the same year Hurricane Katrina came through and tore up everything. It ended up being a great decision after all. I think the way things turned out, I know it was the best decision for me to stay here."

On possibly playing with another team in 2008: "It came pretty close. Actually, I flew down to New York and visited with Jets head coach Eric Mangini and his staff. They were really excited about signing me up and making me a Jet. It was tempting because I had talked to Bill and I knew they weren't going to bring me back here. It was tempting to get out there and see what I could do for one more year. I had to sit back and I thought about it for a long time. That's what has taken me so long to give you the announcement that I was done playing. It just didn't feel right and I didn't want to go somewhere and give someone an effort that I didn't think was acceptable to me; and try to give that to them and say, 'This is what I can give you.' That just wasn't my style. I wasn't going to give them a mediocre performance when I thought I was capable of doing more. I didn't think I was able to provide them with the type of plays that they were probably looking for."

On what sparked him to retire: "I couldn't stop going to Baskin-Robbins. I kind of knew then. When June comes around I am usually on a strict diet. I celebrate my birthday on July 2. Other than that, when June comes around, it's usually collard greens and all that good stuff, baked chicken. When I am still going to Baskin-Robbins, I figured it was probably over."

His reaction when Bill Belichick asked him to play defensive back: "I kind of thought they were joking. I was sitting at my locker and it was a situation where I always used to tease Ty Law about playing defensive back. Ty used to always do the same with receivers coach Brian Daboll about playing receiver. We never really thought anything about it but we did it for years. I was sitting at my locker, looking over my offensive plays, and Eric Mangini comes in and drops this defensive playbook in my face like, 'Get ready to go. You are doing one-on-ones today.' I'm putting on my shoes, getting ready to practice and I'm like, 'How am I supposed to learn this in 10 minutes?' That's how it came about. He came in and said, 'You always said you wanted to play defensive back and you can do it so here's your chance.'"

On the challenge of covering Donald Driver in the 2006 game against Green Bay: "Donald is a pretty explosive and strong player. He catches the ball really well with his hands. I think you guys have seen him play a couple times here in the Monday night games against Dallas. He makes outstanding plays. He's able to accelerate and he knows how to get open. It was a tough task to go up against him and hold him down to one catch like that. Like Bill said, I kind of surprised myself a little bit. When you play guys like that you know that they are going to make some catches and make some plays. That game, he just wasn't able to get going. Maybe it wasn't all me. Maybe it was him a little bit, but he just couldn't get going. Like Bill said it was probably one of the proudest moments of my career as a defensive back in the league."

On what it meant for the coaching staff to trust him with that assignment: "Bill wouldn't have put me on the field if he felt like it was going to be a detriment to his team. You know how Bill is. He's not going to play a guy if a guy says he can play and Bill doesn't think he can play. He's not going to put him on the field. He's not going to jeopardize the success of the rest of the team for the success of one or two guys. When he put me out there, I said, 'He must really believe that I can get this job done'. Or he just didn't have another choice. He was just like, 'You've got to play.' But it turned out well. Having that confidence in me, knowing Bill, that really meant a lot to me. Knowing that he believed that I was smart enough and capable enough to go out there and help the football team win some games."

On the importance of playing for one team his entire career: "I always thought about playing with the same team. It was something that was on my mind for a long time. Being able to stay here and finish up my career, especially once I started getting out a little more, doing some charity work, doing some other business ventures was important to me. I just kind of got planted here. It's tough to pick up and move, leave the area and get started somewhere else. More than anything I love playing for this team. I love playing for the organization and the way that Mr. Kraft has gone about running this team. You hear so many horror stories about organizations not taking care of their players and guys are just out for their own. They have guys working out in trailers. You have guys meeting in barns and you hear about all that stuff and, in some places that was the case. Some guys just didn't have the facilities and they didn't really care about how comfortable the players were. Here, it's been pretty comfortable. We've got one of the best digs in there to get dressed in. You walk out of the back and go to the practice field now. You guys know where I was when I started, I am getting old. You had to drive to practice when I got here, for six, seven, eight years, whatever it was. It was a nightmare having to get in your car and drive over there, get stopped by the train, get fined $50 by Bill Parcells for being late because the train was coming. It was tough coming in here. You had the horses and buggies running around the track and horse poop and all this stuff. Now, you look out there and see what Robert Kraft's done with this place. It's quite amazing. He made it pretty comfortable to be here."

On being part of the revival of the Patriots and if that meant a lot to him: "I think I got a little bit of a taste even though Bill Parcells was already here as the new coach. He had started to make that transition over to being a winning organization but you could still see remnants of the team, the way it used to be and the struggles they had to win. Then Mr. Kraft came in and you could really see the team turn the corner. It all started with the players. Trying to make situations better for the players, serving players breakfast in the morning—something we didn't get our first year. Then we were getting lunch and ultimately three meals a day. I don't have any food in my house if my family's not here. I didn't have to leave; you come in and they can make you a waffle in the mornings, get fresh omelets and scrambled eggs, whatever cereal you want and fruit. Any time of the day you can go in there and eat. I think it started with that, starting to take care of the players more.

"I think Mr. Kraft realized that if you take care of the players they're going to give it back to you. I think that was part of the big turn in the whole situation and obviously getting Bill Belichick to come back here and coach this football team, which a lot of people doubted. He didn't have a lot of success in Cleveland and there are a lot of things that go with that success. Nobody knew what his front office situation was. Nobody knew if he was calling the shots, if he was bringing in the players. I don't know a lot about the coaching business but it's tough. I do remember the whole Parcells thing, about shopping for the groceries or whatever between him and Mr. Kraft. That's the nature of this business but when you get a chance to go out there, get your players, you put them in the right position and you get them to win, teach them how to win, it makes a big difference.

"I think bringing Bill Belichick back in here, teaching football the way he knows how to teach it and the way he knows how to play it—he's been around the game for 30-plus years. I think he's somebody you need to listen to when it comes to learning the game of football. He did a great job of getting the right type of players that he wanted to coach and putting it all together and teaching. He taught the game of football. He didn't just put us out on the field and say 'Run this play.' He taught us the game of football, taught us the way he wanted it done and it ended up being, and still is, quite successful."

His son asking why he's retiring if he loves football so much: "It's something that's out of my control. I would love to keep playing but there comes a time when the man upstairs called God, you can't outrun him as much as you try to and want to. He just catches up to you and tells you that you're 37 years old. Your knee is hurting. Your hip is not in great shape. You can't run as fast as you used to. There's a bunch of 22-year-old guys out there that are taking your place. I'm no longer 22, and in this game there are very few places for guys that are 37 years old.

"Therefore, you have to move on and create other goals and things to achieve and you try to push on and achieve those things. It's a sad day for me too. I saw you out there crying for me and I love you and it's going to be okay. Daddy's still going to be around football and he still loves football. If you want to play football he'll come watch you play and teach you how to play too. As long as you don't get mad at him when I coach you too hard and when I get on you too hard. That's just a part of the game. You get older and you're not able to keep up as well as you used to. Therefore you have to leave the game. I've got more time to sit down and watch it with you, whenever you want to. That's what happens."

Fifteen

IN HIS OWN WORDS:
LIFE AFTER FOOTBALL

Junior's situation got me thinking about
some of the big hits I took over my career.

CHAPTER FIFTEEN

In His Own Words: Life After Football

Retirement and Comebacks: I never had the urge to pull a Brett Favre and come back. I know I feel all right most of the time, but that's just because I'm not doing football workouts. You have no pounding on the joints anymore, so you're feeling pretty good. I know that even if I started thinking about it, I'm sure I'd go out there and have two or three workouts and run routes and start to feel some of those aches and pains again. But you do get that feeling: *Hey, I feel good now.* Then you go out there and run around and you feel the little soreness set in.

What I Miss: I think that's probably the biggest thing about getting older. It takes you a little longer to recover, and the soreness doesn't go away. It doesn't really disappear like it used to anymore. Now, I tell everybody, 'I don't miss it until the playoffs start.' That time of year, my whole body chemistry changes, and I get the chills all over again. I get the anxiety again. I feel the sense of urgency again. It's something I really can't even explain to people. The regular season, man, I didn't really miss it a whole lot at all. If there is something I miss, it's spending time with the guys more than anything else. But that playoff atmosphere, man, is what I really missed about the game.

Those crunch-time situations and having to make a play or do something to get your team over the top or get them in position to help them win a game—I miss picking up the big first down, the big block, big return. Those are the situations that I miss.

But I can sit there and watch a regular season game all day and not even miss it, not one bit. I know a lot of guys that say they didn't watch football for like a whole year after they were done. They go fishing or something. But I would watch almost every game and didn't feel a thing. That first year I was out, the Patriots didn't make the playoffs, but I still got the same feeling. The playoffs started, and you see guys getting ready to play and getting hyped, and listening to fiery players like Ray Lewis getting his team going with motivational speeches. That's when I'd miss it.

What's Next: When I retired, I really didn't have a master plan as to what I wanted to do with the rest of my life. Most of all, I was just kind of tired. I just wanted to go chill out, take a year off and do some fishing and soul searching. But some New England media outlets started calling. I think it was sports radio WEEI who called me first, and then, maybe Comcast SportsNet. I ended up going in and doing a show or two here and there, and I really enjoyed it. I never thought I'd be doing it regularly, because I really didn't like being in front of the cameras too much when I was a player. Not that I didn't like the media, but it just didn't seem like something I'd be interested in doing once I stopped playing. I was a little shy at first, but it's done me a world of good since retiring. I'm not as shy as I used to be, and not afraid of the camera as I used to be. So, it's helped me in terms of dealing with people and getting more comfortable in that setting. I've ended up getting into it and really liking it. I feel like the more I've stuck with it, I've improved.

I didn't think it would be for me, and I was very reluctant to do it in the first place. But the more I've gotten into it, the idea of being able to give my opinion on the sport that I love, football, is a really cool thing. It also provides me with nice flexibility to spend time with my kids. When I was playing during football season, it was tough to do that. You come home, you're tired. You don't want to do much. You're beat up. And they're just so excited to see you and just want you to play outside with them. So retirement has opened up a lot more time to be saying "yes" to them in those situations, and I can take them different places and do things I've always wanted to do with them. While I've considered coaching, I think that would be hard to have the same type of flexibility. That's another reason I like what I'm doing—it keeps me around the game and provides that flexibility. And there are different things to strive for within the field—a lot of different levels to try to work toward.

In addition to that work, I have a connection with Narragansett Beer, which is more business-based. I enjoy working with them, helping them with their brand. It's a win-win situation.

Support: When you're going through retirement, the support of people around you is critical. Over the course of my life I've had a tremendous amount of support from all sorts of friends and family. I've talked about my mom being a huge part of that. I've talked about my kids being a huge part of that. My business manager was fantastic, and really helped me a lot.

I've also gotten that from my wife, even though we've been divorced for a couple of years now. Kim is still a huge part of my life and part of my decision-making process, and we are really good friends now. You learn a lot about yourself after you've got to be home with somebody. And she had a career. When I was playing, she was there, I was here, so it was a little difficult at times. Then you have to be with somebody all the time, and you kind of learn each other. I think a lot of times you see people stay together even though they're not in love anymore, and that's not what I wanted and it wasn't what she wanted. You see people stay together but they're not really together, and that's not what love is supposed to be like. She didn't want that and I didn't want that.

I know a lot of people say, "You got to tough it out." We toughed out. Believe me, we toughed it out. We did a lot to try and make it work, but it just didn't work, so I think it's better.

Kids don't need to be in a house where everybody's not happy, and so in the end, we parted ways. We still take care of the kids, and we actually get along better and we're friends now, probably better friends that we ever were. So, that part of it is great. I remain committed to my family, so that was probably what was disappointing for me, probably one of the biggest disappointments that I've ever had. I failed at something, number one, and letting go of the whole idea of having a traditional family. It's probably one of the biggest disappointments that I've ever dealt with. But we're all happy. And there's still a support system there. She still wishes me well. I can bounce things off of her when it comes to business and family—she's smarter than me, so I'd be crazy not to.

You see so many people that go through it and they don't like each other, and they don't get along, and it's played out in the media and in the public. But luckily that wasn't the case with us. It all got resolved in a very diplomatic way. She was a big part of my life, and had a big role in everything that happened. We went through all this stuff together, and that was a fantastic time.

Patriot Pride: In my life, I've been very lucky. I never played for any other team other than the Patriots. I had three different head coaches: two who were pretty similar (Bill Parcells and Bill Belichick), and one a little bit different. It was special playing for the Patriots. I've had the chance to talk with a lot of the guys who have played in different places around the league, and they say it's just different being with a franchise like New England. First, playing for the fans of New England was always a privilege. I think that they appreciated and recognized the hard work and the dedication and the loyalty I had toward the football team and they returned that feeling to me. I was a blue-collar player in a white-collar state, and I think they liked that.

When it comes to the Patriots, the push toward excellence and the dedication and commitment to being the best player and the best team is unsurpassed. Just becoming the best team you could become was a daily exercise. I don't think you find the attention to detail at other places is anything close to what it is here in New England. You really get entrenched into the game of football here. You can see it when other guys come here, and when they really can't handle the pressure that's put on them, the expectations that are placed upon them here. There's a lot of pressure and a lot of responsibility put upon them when they come to New England, and they are held accountable for it by their coaches. There are a lot of people out there that might not like Bill Belichick and a lot of players that didn't like Bill Parcells because they held them accountable. And when they were told about it, if they didn't step up to the plate and handle their business the way they were supposed to, then they were gone.

That's what I looked for as a player, and that's what every player should want: feedback. I don't want you to always tell me I'm great at something, or even just okay, when really you're thinking something different. Tell me what you really think, and I'll make the adjustments the best I can. I don't think a lot of people can or could handle that from Parcells or Belichick. And those are the reasons why I love those two. Not to say that I agree with everything that they've always done and the way they've operated, but I've learned. I've sat back and watched them, and I've learned from the mistakes and I've learned from the things I thought they did really well, too. That's what's important. At the end of the day, everything is about the learning process. You learn from your mistakes. You learn from all of it; and you grow from it.

Concussions: Some have asked me what I think about football and some of the issues facing the game, such as concussions and head trauma. A former teammate, the late great Junior Seau, committed suicide two years after his retirement and he suffered from chronic brain damage, some specialists concluded.

As a player, Junior was unique and someone I always respected, even before he joined the Patriots in 2006 and was playing for the San Diego Chargers and Miami Dolphins. The intensity with which he played the game made an impression on me, that look in his eyes, you could see how much he lived to be in those situations and craved winning. He put all he had every play and that's really the way he was off the field, too. He was always full of energy, had great instincts, and his passion was infectious. He delivered a real spark for us, which included pre-game speeches. Sometimes he got so worked up, you couldn't really understand what he was saying, but we all got the point. A teammate might look to another and say, "I don't know what the heck Junior just said, but I'm ready to go out there and run through a wall right now!" Such intensity for the game can't be fake, and it's hard to replicate. On top of that, he was always happy and a real joy to be around. He had his acoustic guitar in the locker room and played it all the time. That led some other players to get their own guitars, such as defensive lineman Richard Seymour, who talked about how relaxing it was. Sometimes it felt like we were all around a campfire with Junior when he was talking about having fun or playing his Zac Brown Band music.

One specific memory with Junior for me was being at his golf tournament in California and we had a discussion about staying positive about things. He never had any bad things to say, and he talked about how people liked to tear other people down when they are going through something difficult. He turned to me and said, "We've got to help these people out. We've got to prop them up, be a friend." Those were the types of things he'd talk about a lot, so it was a shock to me when he committed suicide. He was going through serious stuff himself that none of us were really aware of.

Junior's situation got me thinking about some of the big hits I took over my career. Thankfully, I haven't had many major issues. I'm still pretty healthy for my age. Probably the biggest hit I took was in the late 1990s in a game against the Dolphins, and it was delivered by linebacker Zach Thomas. I was coming over the middle, trying to make a catch on a quick slant and the pass was a little high. Zach, who was so instinctive, kind of baited us to throw it in my direction by turning his shoulders the opposite way and then came back to the ball. Because the pass was so high, I just couldn't protect myself. He hit me, and boom! I was just gone. I had no idea what had happened. The last thing I remember was just coming off the line of scrimmage.

There is a lot of talk about player safety and when I think about that play, having my mouthpiece was critical. I had a custom-made piece that snapped onto my bottom teeth and that ensured my teeth would never hit together on situations like that. When I absorbed that hit from Zach Thomas, my tongue sort of came out of my mouth, between my teeth, and if I didn't have the mouth guard in I could have bitten it right off. That's how significant the impact was. I couldn't eat for a week after that, couldn't even taste my food. I was drinking milkshakes and my tongue was black, blue and purple for a week. That was one time I remember my mother being upset, and that's always hard as a player because you want your loved ones watching to know you're okay. But the truth is that I wasn't; I don't remember it all too well. So I'm a big advocate of mouthpieces.

My mentality as a player was always to do whatever I needed to do to get back on the field. We had some other injured players that week, and they needed me. I kept thinking to myself on the sideline, "Can I go back in? Should I go back in?" As a player, you never really want to let your teammates or coaches down so the answer for me was usually "Yes, put me in." But that was one day I remember I never should have been back in the game. I couldn't stop my hands from shaking and I was actually pretty scared. I had jitters and was doing everything I could to try to slow things down, taking deep breaths, and all I could hope for was that the football wouldn't come in my direction. I didn't know if I could catch it with my hands shaking like that, and my blocking was affected.

I made it through the rest of that game and I don't blame anyone for that. Those types of situations were commonplace at the time and we're much more aware of those things now, with mandatory, independent concussion tests. Those are important because it takes the decision out of the player's hands. Most players didn't want to take themselves out or they might be considered soft.

When you sign up to play this game, you know you're going to get hit. I knew there was a possibility to blow out my knee or injure my shoulder. I was fine with that and I remember signing a document at some point that actually said something like "football can be hazardous to your health." I don't want to sound insensitive to some of the difficult situations that some former players now find themselves in, and my heart goes out to them all, but it was all pretty clear to me.

The way I always looked at it was, "I know these are the dangers of football. This is what could possibly happen to me, and I'm going to give it a shot anyway." It's not much different from the everyday worker who could be injured based on what they do—those who work on the highway, loggers, miners. Back in the day, it was black lung that killed so many people. So there's an element of danger to a lot of the jobs that are out there. And as long as those dangers are laid out on the table for you, and there's nothing being hidden away from you, then it's your decision to pursue that job. And that's the thing I'm saying about the older players now—if certain things weren't disclosed to them, they have an argument and a half. If they had no idea what they were getting themselves into, then there's an argument.

The league has cracked down on some of the big hits, increasing the number of on-field penalties and off-field financial fines for them, and I haven't always agreed with them. But given where the game is today, with many former players filing lawsuits against the league, the NFL probably feels it has to make a strong statement and stick with it in hopes of changing the game. I think a key is starting with the young kids so they grow up playing that way from the start.

But I think that people have to come to terms with the fact that there's going to be a certain level of violence in the game. It's just part of the sport, and you have to come to terms with it. I don't think they're going to ban football anytime soon. There are too many jobs and too much money in it. And it's a great form of entertainment. Have you seen the television ratings?

I'm sure there are going to be a lot more safety changes coming, and hopefully, there's somebody out there who can make some equipment that will reduce concussions. The challenge will be trying to do that while keeping the interests of the public and keeping the NFL the No. 1 sports and entertainment option around. People love watching football—I love watching football—but for me as a fan, there's still an aspect of getting used to it with the new rules. It makes it a lot harder on defensive players.

While I was playing, there wasn't a whole lot of change in how concussions were treated. I think right after I retired, you started hearing about that if a guy was dinged or concussed, then he wasn't coming back, and that was it. Some players, like Pittsburgh Steelers wide receiver Hines Ward, got really upset when he couldn't get back into the game. You didn't see that type of stuff when I was playing. A player who might have had a concussion usually wasn't listed that way on the injury report. They would say it was a shoulder injury or a stinger. So I do think the league is going in the right direction in the light of everything that's happened; there are things happening to guys who I've played with, and they are struggling with their mental and physical health. I know that sometimes it's more than just football they're struggling with—Corwin Brown, Kevin Turner, and Ted Johnson are three who come to mind.

It's a little scary for me as a former player and it makes me feel like I've been extremely fortunate after playing 15 seasons. I haven't experienced any thoughts or had any crazy things that have gone through my head where I want to do harm to myself or anybody else. And I'm praying I never do. One thing the league could do is to help out more with insurance once players are out of the game and help pay for the services they may have incurred when they were playing. I had great insurance when I played and through the early years of my retirement, but when you get to the point where you no longer have that, it's hard to find something comparable. So I don't know if former players can find the same level of care they had when they were playing. I'd like to be able to purchase the same plan that I had with the league when I was a player. That would make a big difference as you never know who may need counseling.

When the Game's Over: I feel as if the league is doing more to help out guys when it comes to off-field stuff. For examples, rookies entering the league have a symposium and they talk about a lot of those issues. With the Patriots, we had people come in and talk about life off the field from time to time. Harold Nash, who is the Patriots' head strength and conditioning coach, was doing it for a while with the team. They bring in financial advisors, they bring in speakers—a lot of things to get guys ready for life after football, such as entrepreneur programs, where they're sending guys to school on tuition reimbursement programs. So they have a lot of things in place but one of the problems is that guys don't always see that door closing on them until it's completely shut. For me, football was a huge part of my life for 30 years, and I didn't think I'd be anything else. I probably thought I wanted to go into coaching and I was lucky. But this game can be finished for anyone, on any day, or any time. I don't think you know when you run out of gas. I would have played forever if I could have.

Part of the challenge post-retirement is losing the structure of football. It can be tough to wrap your head around what you want to do next. It's like my whole life has been structured and organized, and everything had to be a certain time. I had to be back here for training camp in August, get ready for the season in September, arrive at a certain time, leave at a certain time—it's all rigid and many decisions are made for you. There is comfort in that routine and it's almost like you're running on autopilot. And all of a sudden, you don't have that anymore. If you haven't prepared yourself to do anything else after football, it's going to be real, real, real tough.

Then there's the whole issue if your self-esteem is tied to your playing career. You hear some retired players say, "It's not the same as when you were playing; people look at you different and you don't have the same status." That's true in many cases, but the key is obviously to not let the fact that you played in the league define who you are. That is easier said than done in some cases, but there's going to be people shuffling in all the time, and there's going to be a hot new star every year. That's just the way the system works. It's the same in music and movies. There are new people shuffling in all the time, but you can't let that define who you are, because if somebody treats you different than they did when you were playing, then you don't need to be associated with that person anyway.

I've been lucky enough to be able to fill that void. I spend a lot of time with my kids. I'm always staying busy, and during the season, I'm talking football either on the radio or on TV. I'm not making $1 million a year, but I'm enjoying what I do, and the people I work with, and the things I'm talking about. I'm comfortable with my situation. Figuring out how to successfully transition out of the game is a big concern for a lot of players and I feel fortunate. But if I was commissioner, I'd try to help. And I think they're doing that now, trying to help players understand that some future planning can put themselves in positions where they can be successful. I'd say that if you want to implement real change in the game, start with some of these college kids, and even high school kids, to get the message across to them. Eliminate that sense of entitlement you see in so many young players.

You need to start preparing now, because the NFL could last one day, it could last 15 years. It's like they say "NFL stands for Not For Long." I would promote a program where I'd talk to high school coaches, maybe even middle school coaches, and encourage the thought that kids need to stop getting free passes, and there needs to be a level of accountability. I've seen too many times where a very good athlete gets in a position where they're probably going to fail, or they're going to flunk a class, or they're going to get in trouble for something crazy they did, but they get a free pass and are allowed to keep playing just because they're good at sports. But that player needs to be held accountable for that at that time. The end result is that when you make it to the NFL, or the NBA, or the major leagues, they've been given everything they've got and never really had to earn anything. And then we want to ask the question, "Why is this kid the way he is when he gets to that level?"

Go back to his past and that might help explain it. It all ties in together. So the idea is to start planting that seed early, because I think that's really what happens to a lot of our athletes is that we're never held accountable for anything. If you're any good, you often have to do something very drastic to get thrown off a team, or to get kicked out of school, or to serve a suspension. And kids know that. They know what they can get away with and what they cannot get away with. And you don't think that he won't make that same mistake again as an adult? Or if he makes it to the NBA, or to the NFL, that he won't end up broke? Nip it in the bud now and send that message now that you have to be accountable. You have to be able to do your math, so you can keep up with your account and know what you're spending and bringing in. And be accountable now. It isn't that hard to do—to send a message.

I'm not sure how to make that all happen, but the NFL should be leading the charge. If high schools and middle schools see the league taking that approach, maybe they follow suit. I know it's probably naïve to a degree, especially with the big money in college sports, so maybe it's a dream scenario. But accountability is the first thing that comes to mind.

Another issue that is a little more personal to me is the condition of the playing fields. My knee became an issue late in my career and I do wonder if I had played on natural grass if it might have been different. So I'd encourage all NFL teams to keep natural grass playing surfaces. This artificial turf is not for me. If you fall down and hit your head on artificial turf, it's a hard surface that can do damage. So if we're serious as a league about player safety, we'd bring back grass to every stadium and practice facility.

One other thing is that I know the league has really worked hard to protect quarterbacks (especially when it comes to blows to the head), but we still need to protect guys and their knees at other positions. You're starting to see more and more rules passed with this in mind, and I think that's a good thing. There are a lot of other guys out there who have their livelihood wrapped up in their knees. You're allowed to go in and cut a guy down at the knees and tackle a guy at the knees. I understand the reality of the situation, how the quarterbacks drive the league and they make it popular, and that's why you put them out front. But let's give everybody else some protection and an equal opportunity to make as much as they can make while they're here. I feel like the league continues to move a bit more in that direction.

Sixteen

PATRIOTS HALL
OF FAMER

We had our problems here and there,
but for the most part we handled
our business the Patriot Way.

CHAPTER SIXTEEN

Patriots Hall of Famer

When Troy was inducted into the Patriots Hall of Fame in 2012, in his first year of eligibility, he opened his remarks to those in attendance at the official ceremony by saying, "I love you too." And then he asked where his mother, Richadean, was sitting in the crowd.

The following was the beginning of his speech:

"We came, we saw, we conquered. Yes we did. A Patriot is one who loves his or her country, or team, and supports its best interests. Patriotism—love for, or devotion, to one's country or to your team. I'm done."

And with that, Troy pretended, for a moment, to walk off the stage. Everyone laughed.

Then he continued, later taking a humorous break about halfway through the speech to apply lip balm provided by receiver Deion Branch.

"Let me thank each and every one of you out here, for being here today. I appreciate it tremendously. I can think back to 1993 and trust me, this was the last thing on my mind, standing behind this podium and talking about being in the Patriots Hall of Fame. It's not that I didn't believe in my abilities or what I was capable of doing. It just seemed like it was hard to get traction to start my career. As hard as Scott Zolak fought to get me the ball in the early days of my career, it didn't seem to work out. But I'm glad to be standing here today.

"I've had a lot of love and a lot of support from a lot of people, a lot of fans, coaches, and teammates along the way. I want to thank you right now, because it is greatly appreciated and it will never be forgotten.

"I didn't forget about you, Momma. As we do at all these things, you can't forget about Momma. I get asked the question a lot, 'What made you want to do this?' Or 'What made you want to play defense?' When I talk about my mother, she is one of the most unselfish people that you'll ever come across in your life. We didn't have a lot, couldn't do a lot of things, but if she had a dollar more than the next person and that person needed it, she would give it up. That's the kind of heart she has. She not only raised me, my brother and sister, but she was the oldest girl of nine kids and she sacrificed a lot to help her mother raise those kids. She was my mother and she was my father when he was absent from my life. She did a very good job of teaching me the Patriot Way. It started early on.

"I'm not going to cry. My brother, my sister—Dwayne, Nene—I love you dearly. I know I can get on your nerves sometimes and you get to see a side of me that not everyone gets to see. I've given you some flak from time to time, but I love you for all the support you've shown over the years, continuing to show up. Any awards and praise that I do receive, you are more excited than I am, jumping up and down, being excited, wondering when they might be coming back to

New England to celebrate something. So hopefully that will be at the end of the season this year.

"All the other family members who are here, thank you also for all the support. I also want to thank a very special person that was in my life, Kim. She gave me two of the most beautiful gifts that anyone could give any human being—Sir'mon and SaanJay—my two sons. I could never, ever thank her enough for that. Sir'mon and SaanJay, you continue to be my drive and inspiration to do great things with the rest of my life. When I played, I looked for you in the stands and always gave you my signal. You remembered. My two boys; I know how hard it was for you when I retired and had to leave the game. You thought I was leaving New England for good. We would never leave here. We'll always be a part of this place. I just hope you continue to do well in school and then you can go on to do great things. Thank you, boys.

"My high school and my little league years, I have to thank all my coaches from that era. My high school coach, Tim Moore, had me early on. Mike Pope, who still continues to do camps all around the country for offensive linemen. He is a double amputee and he continues to volunteer his time, from state to state, high school to high school, doing coaches' clinics. He's a great man, a hard-working man, and he's the one who really got me introduced to the passing game and offenses when I was in high school.

"The guys who had me in college at Marshall; Chris Scelfo recruited me, he's now coaching in the NFL. Coach Jim Donnan and Mark Gale, a guy who bent over backwards to do everything he could to get my transcripts from one school to the next when I was taking summer school courses. Even though they aren't here today, I want to thank them. Those guys were probably the ones who opened my eyes that I could possibly play pro football. If it wasn't for Coach Donnan, knowing Bill Parcells at the time, I probably wouldn't be standing here right now because he had the connection and told Bill to give me the chance.

"Bill Parcells, I know we had our disagreements from time to time and didn't always agree on everything. But I'll tell you this, he gave me what I always asked for and the only thing I ever asked for—an opportunity. He pushed me, he pulled me, talked junk to me; Ty Law would attest to that. I wish I had the mouth that Ty had, but he respected it all. And Drew Bledsoe can tell you too, he was a hard man, a tough man, but I think it helped shape us all to be what we became.

"Probably the greatest of all time, I have to give a huge, huge thank you to Bill Belichick. That coaching staff, with offensive coordinator Charlie Weis, I don't know what it was they saw in me…I don't know if it was that they saw me keep grinding. I heard Drew Bledsoe telling a story last night about me working out, doing all kinds of crazy things, jumping rope, whatever it was. I remember when Robert Kraft hired Bill Belichick in 2000, one of the first things Coach Belichick did was call me and tell me he wanted to give me an opportunity to be a starting receiver for the New England Patriots. He went even further the next year, in 2001, when he decided to suspend Terry Glenn for the entire season, after he had been suspended for the first four games. That really gave me the confidence that he believed in what I could do, and my talents. That cemented my career for me, and I do appreciate that.

"I stand here before this Hall of Fame sign, and all this beautiful stuff that fans have to enjoy—like chair-back seats in the stadium, high-definition big screens, CBS Scene, you even have a medical facility on campus here, the dining hall for players is immaculate. This crowd, in 1991, we would have never got this. In 1992, we would have never got this. In 1993, maybe half of the people would be here. But now, from what Mr. Robert Kraft and what his family has been able to build for all of us Patriots to come back and enjoy whenever we have a chance to do it—he has done a tremendous job building this and the Patriots into one of the most profitable franchises in the NFL.

"I remember 1994, when your beloved Myra Kraft saw me feeding the fish at training camp at Bryant University, and she thought it looked like I needed a hug. Maybe it was that we could see each other eye to eye, but she took a liking to me. Maybe that's why you kept me around so long. I love her dearly for that, I love you guys dearly for that. Be proud of what you've been able to build here and the way you've done it—with pride, dignity, and always first-class.

"I don't want to leave anyone out, so I'm going to do something that I saw Curtis Martin do. All the players who played before me, before 1993, please stand up. I have a tremendous amount of respect for you. I appreciate and honor and will never let anybody forget about what you guys did for the New England Patriots and the National Football League. We are the No. 1 sport, by far now, because of what you were able to build. Not great benefits back then, not great pay; I've talked to some of you about how you had second jobs when you played. There was no off-season training. Now we have young kids who can market themselves and make all kinds of money off the football field,

I won't let them forget who built the foundation for them to do that. It was you.

"And now, all the guys who played with me from 1993 and into future years, please stand up. What a good-looking group of guys right there. I want to thank each and every one of you for everything you helped me accomplish in my career. All the headbutts that Tedy Bruschi gave me, all the encouragement that Drew Bledsoe gave me. Ty Law, all the battles in practice until he decided to take a play off here or there; we had a little buddy system going. Trust me, I had a tremendous amount of pleasure, and I really enjoyed playing with you guys; I wouldn't be standing here if it wasn't for the efforts of guys like yourself being such great football players and having such a great mentality for the game, and an attitude and respect for the game that you have. I thank you very much for that. I appreciate it.

"One thing Bill Belichick said to our team a long time ago was that there is an 'I' in team, because your team is made up of individuals doing their jobs. If you let the rest of your teammates down by not doing your job, then the whole thing is going to be a complete failure. So when I look at these guys down here, and think about how we were able to go to five Super Bowls together and win three of them, we had to be on the same page. We had to be on the same wavelength. Something was clicking with us, because we helped each other tremendously throughout the years. I think about how I went on defense, and there was always encouragement. It was always a positive attitude in that locker room. We had our problems here and there, but for the most part we handled our business the Patriot Way. We valued that 'I'—getting ourselves ready—to benefit the entire team.

"Guys who aren't here, like Shawn Jefferson, Sam Gash, the guys from the early 1990s. Andre Tippett—you introduced me to the world of the National Football League in 1993, my rookie season. I was like, 'Wow.' He came into Pittsburgh's locker room and I couldn't move after seeing what he did to that place; he's like a fifth-degree black belt. I don't know if you've ever tried to kick over a five-gallon water cooler full of Gatorade or water, but he did it to five or six of them. Turned over trunks, knocked over lockers, stuff was flying all over the place and I'm thinking 'What have I got myself into? Just don't come down this end.' That's the reason they had to build Heinz Field. I saw Coach Parcells come in the door and turn back around.

"I want to thank my agent, Gary Uberstine, for helping me throughout the end part of my career, to make the transition from being a football player to a regular old guy out in the crowd. I appreciate all the advice and mentorship you gave me.

"Last but not least, you the fans. You've always supported me and treated me like I was a native New Englander. I'm also honored I was able to spend my entire career here in the red, white, and blue of the New England Patriots. You can be tough on us, but I appreciated it, and got to know who you are. When you were happy, you let us know it. When you were unhappy, you let us know it. But I embraced it because it forced us to work harder to get you to cheer for us and get behind us. We could be 14–1, get down 20–0, and we'd get booed. But that's all right. It made us work a little harder. But you could be intimidating to the other team when you needed to be. I remember the Colts coming in here, opening night, and you were intimidating. I remember the 2003 playoff game when we shut down Peyton Manning. So don't ever forget, when you're out in the stands, you are the 12th man, holding us accountable and pushing us to be our best.

"To receive the most [Patriots Hall of Fame] votes out of anybody, next to Drew Bledsoe, I don't know what to say other than thank you for so much love and support for all these years. You sat up there in the aluminum bleachers, cold, yelling and screaming for us, supporting us. I do appreciate it from the bottom of my heart.

"And Momma, again, thank you for teaching me to do things the Patriot Way early in my life. My teammates, fans, owners, and coaches—we came, we saw it, and we conquered it! Thank you very much."

AFTERWORD

BY TROY BROWN

These last two Super Bowl wins, over the Seattle Seahawks and Atlanta Falcons, couldn't have been any more dramatic for the Patriots.

Up to that point, I felt like even though they hadn't won it in 10 years, they were still the most consistent franchise in NFL history. They were always competitive, always had a chance to be in almost every single game, consistently in the playoffs.

You watched as a bunch of players signed contracts with them through the years, for the chance to compete and win a Super Bowl. So winning those two Super Bowls solidified them at least as the greatest modern-day team. I know Pittsburgh has six Super Bowls in its history, but we haven't seen any run like this in the salary-cap, free-agent era.

In Super Bowl LI against the Falcons, it's 28–3 in the third quarter and things don't look good for the Patriots. But being around the team, you know to never say the game is over. I could see the calm on Coach Belichick's face when they flashed to him on the sideline. That was a sign to me that there was no panic despite the lopsided score. It was similar when looking at Tom Brady.

The main thing I was thinking about is whether they would run out of time. I'm not going to lie; I was a little worried watching it, especially after the Falcons scored quickly after halftime, which makes you question whether the right adjustments were made.

As a former player, you feel a little helpless. There's nothing you can do to help even though you're feeling that urgency.

Then the tide starts to turn, and I'm thinking to myself, "If Atlanta doesn't understand how this game is played down the stretch, they're going to lose." You could see how they didn't understand how the Super Bowl was played, how to maximize TV timeouts and all those things. It started to catch up with them, and then you look at the end of it and the Patriots have run almost double the number of plays on offense. It caught up to the Falcons. Some of their play-calling was suspect.

In that situation, you could see what everybody who has been in the Patriots franchise since 1993 has experienced: How the teaching and coaching and having players ready for those kinds of moments benefits them. They handled the situations much better than the Falcons. It obviously helps when you have a coach like Bill Belichick and a quarterback like Tom Brady. But you also have to give a lot of the other players credit for stepping up in those tough situations to outmaneuver their opponent when they had to.

That goes back to the start of the season when they had to play without Brady for the first four games because of the NFL suspension he was serving. It interested me how Brady got away from everything for those four weeks, just going out and enjoying that time. His mother, Galynn, had been ill, so he got to spend time with her.

The Patriots went 3–1 without Brady and it easily could have been 4–0. The one loss, 16–0 to the Buffalo Bills, came after top backup Jimmy Garoppolo had injured his shoulder and you could tell that rookie Jacoby Brissett wasn't ready to run the same type of offense and was playing through a finger injury that also affected him. That's still a pretty impressive performance by a football team that didn't have Brady under center. It reflects a team with a lot of talented football players on it.

Fast-forward to 2017 and it looks like they've improved from that point. So it's no wonder that expectations are high.

At the same time, the 2017 team hasn't done anything at this point. So while I hear some of the comparisons between the 2017 team and the 2007 team, and this team is extremely talented, I had the pleasure of seeing that '07 team up close from behind the scenes. That was my final year and the talent on that team was impressive: Randy Moss, Donte Stallworth, Jabar Gaffney. Defensively, the line was stacked. You had Mike Vrabel at linebacker, Rodney Harrison at safety, guys that had been around the block a few times. So I'm not putting the '17 team in that category yet.

As for Brady, as he turns 40 before the 2017 regular season, I can't say I'm surprised at how well he's still playing because he's worked his butt off over the years, and has since Day 1 when he first stepped in the building.

It had been 10 years since he won a Super Bowl—he had come close in a couple Super Bowls against the New York Giants—but to see him back on top of the mountain again was great. You almost wondered after those losses to the Giants if maybe it wasn't meant to be. Then all of a sudden they get over the hump in Super Bowl XLIX, get another one in Super Bowl LI, and anyone that had questions about how good Brady truly is couldn't really ask that anymore. The questions had gone away.

I'd argue that there shouldn't have been any question after the first three Super Bowls, but these last two put it all over the top. We can now stop talking about who is the greatest quarterback of all-time.

Now the question is how much longer Brady might play. The way he looked in 2016, he might make it to 45 years old.

Another part of what stood out from the 2016 season was the connection between the fans and Brady. He handled the situation well and his jerseys sold at levels that matched and exceeded every other player, which reflected to me that many realized he shouldn't have been put in that situation by the NFL. As a former teammate, that was difficult to watch him go through, and hear players from other teams bring things up that disparaged the Patriots. At the same time, it was interesting to watch him embrace social media more, and show more of his personality.

So you had the Brady storyline, and before that, what else can be said about cornerback Malcolm Butler and his Super Bowl–saving interception from two years earlier?

Butler is a very confident guy, he reacts well to the ball, makes plays, and fights through to the end of every play. People forget he wasn't even playing on defense in the first half of Super Bowl XLIX, but then the coaching staff called on him in the second half. They had practiced the play and he reacts to it. We're talking about an undrafted corner from West Alabama in that situation coming up with the biggest play in franchise history; at least the biggest until Julian Edelman made that catch in Super Bowl LI.

That's a credit to the Patriots, recognizing what certain guys are able to do in certain situations, and who is going to come through for you when the pressure is on.

When you think about the time I first joined the franchise in 1993, it's hard to believe what has happened. I think they potentially have a few more Super Bowls in them, and obviously everyone asks the question of how much longer Belichick will coach and Brady will play. But I also think they have enough coaches on staff who have been around to keep things going—maybe not at the same level, but enough to keep the torch lit—as well as two young quarterbacks who have shown they are capable of compartmentalizing and leading a team to victories.

Belichick is 65 and it's hard to know how much longer he wants to do this. He's spent his entire life around the game, and it's hard to imagine him not being around it. It won't seem right looking on the sideline and him not being there, whenever that time comes. Still, I'm sure the franchise will still have his ear on certain issues.

One of the words you've heard a lot in recent years with the Patriots is "culture." It means a lot, and the atmosphere you cultivate permeates from top to bottom; it's something everybody feels. It gets to the point where you can do things, and get people moving in the right direction, without as much effort as maybe you had to in the past. You work like a champion, you prepare like a champion. It's a problem when you have to constantly remind guys to do that, but I think it's at a point now where when players enter the building, they automatically feel that change.

There wasn't a lot of success when I first joined the Patriots. They had the '85 team, which went to the Super Bowl, but more down years than good ones to the point that they were kind of the laughingstock of the league. Just about every player I came in with didn't even really realize where New England was, where the team was located. Many ridiculed them.

Scott Zolak, a backup quarterback at the time, had been a hero of sorts because he stepped in to play in 1992 and helped lead the team to its only victories that year. So the expectations of what people were getting from their football team around New England, the bar was set pretty low. That changed after they hired Bill Parcells in 1993 and drafted quarterback Drew Bledsoe. The excitement was growing, it was back to the Super Bowl in '96, and that was sort of the foundation for what we see today.

It's a credit to the fans, too, as Patriots games have all been sold out since 1994. Now you take a poll of the fans about professional sports in the region and the Patriots are probably the most popular franchise in New England. That's hard to do when you consider the Red Sox, Celtics, and Bruins, and their storied histories. But football is probably the number one sport in New England right now.

—Troy Brown
May 2017

ACKNOWLEDGMENTS

I would like to thank my family: my mother, Richadean; my brother, Dwayne; my sister, Nene; and all my aunts, uncles, cousins, nieces, and nephews; Kim, the mother of my children; and especially my sons, Sir'mon and SaanJay; who have always been there to support me in good times and bad and made me strive to be a better man. I hope I've made them proud.

To the countless teammates that I have played with along the way—in high school, college, and the NFL—who have helped me achieve my many successes, either by working with me on my skills, teaching me how to be a professional, or setting an example. Football is the ultimate team sport and I wouldn't have been half the player I was without them.

My Pop Warner and high school football coaches, specifically Mike Pope and Tim Moore, who saw my desire to play, taught me the game, and helped me develop a true appreciation of football.

The coaches at Marshall University, specifically coach Chris Scelfo and head coach Jim Donnan, who saw beyond my physical limitations and took a chance on me, truly believing in me and planting the seeds of confidence.

I would like to thank my off-the-field support system, including my agents, my financial advisors, and personal assistant/business manager, who I depend on and look to for so many things.

Coach Parcells, Coach Belichick, and all the other coaches in the NFL who gave me an opportunity. They helped me take my talents to the next level and be an integral part of three championship teams. Their impact on my life is immeasurable.

To Robert Kraft and the entire Kraft family, specifically Myra, for taking a liking to a young man who was a little out of place, and helping him feel at home, giving him the confidence to succeed. As well as for going out and putting together a championship team and instilling in all of us that we were winners. Those championships wouldn't have been possible without you.

—Troy Brown
May 2015

* * *

My hope with this book is that Troy's remarkable career is given its due, and that those who read it get a true feeling for a terrific underdog story. So the first person to thank is Troy himself. You did all the hard work and I admire you for that.

Chris Price, a local sportswriter who is one of the kindest people, played a major role in this book. Chris provided the framework for the text with his attention to detail and terrific interviewing skills. What I hope for Chris, his wife Kate, and their son Noah is that someone reads this book and sees the remarkable work that Kate is doing to raise awareness on child sex trafficking. Kate is on Twitter at @kpadvocacy.

The always-helpful Patriots media relations staff, with Stacey James, Aaron Salkin, Christy Berkery, Michael Jurovaty, Cecily Faenza, Jeremie Smith, and Travis Basciotta, consistently assists in doing whatever they can to make the job easier. Matt Smith, the executive producer of the Kraft Sports Group, is a close friend who went above and beyond to help. And if not for *Patriots Football Weekly* editor in chief Fred Kirsch, I might not be a football writer today. He gave me my first job covering the sport in 1997.

Ben Rawitz and Tom Brady delivered in the clutch, and for a rookie author, working with Tom Bast, Jesse Jordan, and Triumph Books was a true pleasure. I'm also most appreciative for support from Patricia Mays and ESPN.com's editorial team for providing me the opportunity to take on this career challenge.

Finally, to my wife Sigalle, daughter Talia, and son Nathan, I appreciate every day we have together and the understanding you show when work sometimes takes me away from home—both physically and mentally. Nothing makes me happier than the three of you, and I look forward to where life's journey takes us next.

—Mike Reiss
May 2015